Fishing for Brookies, Browns & Bows

Fishing for
Brookies

With an Intelligent Commentary by  Paul Quarrington

Browns & Bows

The Old Guy's Complete Guide to Catching Trout

GREYSTONE BOOKS

DOUGLAS & MCINTYRE PUBLISHING GROUP

VANCOUVER/TORONTO/NEW YORK

For my best fishing buddy, Sheila

Greystone Books
A division of Douglas & McIntyre Ltd.
2323 Quebec Street, Suite 201
Vancouver, British Columbia
Canada V5T 4S7
www.greystonebooks.com

National Library of Canada Cataloguing in Publication Data
Deval, Gord, 1930–
    Fishing for brookies, browns & bows

    ISBN 1-55054-881-6

    1. Trout fishing. I. Title
SH687.D48 2001   799.1'757   C2001-911045-6

Library of Congress data is available

Editing by Nancy Flight
Jacket and text design and jacket photo-illustration by Peter Cocking
Jacket photo by Tony Makepeace
Interior illustrations by Peter Eastwood
Printed and bound in Canada by Friesens
Printed on acid-free paper ∞

We gratefully acknowledge the financial support of the Canada Council
for the Arts, the British Columbia Ministry of Tourism, Small Business
and Culture, and the Government of Canada through the Book Publishing
Industry Development Program (BPIDP) for our publishing activities.

Contents

. . . .

Introduction *by Paul Quarrington* 1
Prologue 14

Part 1 Brook Trout

One The Aristocratic Brookie   24
Two Fishing for Brookies with Live Bait   38
Three Catching Brookies on Artificial Lures   53
Four Fishing for Brookies with Fur & Feather   69
Five Ice Fishing for Brookies   103

Part 2 Brown Trout

One The Reclusive & Elusive Brown Trout   118
Two Fishing for Browns with Live Bait   122
Three Fishing for Browns with Artificials   147
Four Fly-Fishing for Browns   152

Part 3 Rainbow Trout

One The Pot o' Gold   172
Two The Spring Steelhead Run   177
Three Summer Bows   191
Four Ice Fishing for Bows   206

Epilogue 215
Glossary of Fishing Terms & Gordisms   221
Index 230

Introduction

by PAUL QUARRINGTON

. . . .

The book you are holding in your hands was written by my Old Guy.

You don't know how lucky you are, on a couple of counts. You're lucky to have the Old Guy's special knowledge bundled up and glued between cardboard so that you might ever refer to it. You can dog-ear the really good parts. I suggest you immediately go to page 84 and turn down the corner there, where it tells you how to make Despairs. You're going to be making a lot of them, I'll bet, because it is the Old Guy's favourite fly and therefore likely the most effective trout fly in the world.

But you are also lucky to have this book because it means that you don't have to deal with *him*. Don't get me wrong, I like the Old Guy, but dealing with him can be something of a challenge.

I detailed our relationship in *Fishing With My Old Guy*. I was thinking that for the purposes of this introduction I might simply summarize what I wrote there, but then I decided (a) that's a bit lazy and (b) if I did, you, dear reader, might not be tempted to go out and purchase your own copy of *Fishing With*

My Old Guy. So instead I am going to set out, in some detail, a day spent with the Old Guy.

You shall see exactly what dealing with him is like.

The day begins early, shortly after 4:00 A.M. That is not long after I've gone to bed. Indeed, the coffee I put on when I retired has only just now finished brewing, so I stumble down to the kitchen and consume a mug. The day I'm describing takes place in early May, so the night outside is dark and bone-chilling. I climb into long underwear and put on jeans and a thick shirt. I don my fishing jacket, which is hideously ugly but utilitarian. The garment is, basically, a bunch of pockets stitched together, and into these pockets I put my gear. I have a little plastic box full of lures: Mepps and Vibraxes, numbers 2 and 3, a couple of 4s. I have a number of plastic bags. I have a little knife. I have a set of nail clippers cleverly attached to the zipper of my fishing jacket, where they can get in my way all day long. Then I put on my fishing hat, which I think began life as a fedora but now should be grateful even to be on someone's head, that's how un-hatlike it has become. The hat is also festooned with trout flies (the aforementioned Despair is well represented). I'll wager you thought that anglers wore flies in their headgear for handier access, didn't you? I'm here to tell you that these lures will never be removed from that hat; I believe that the final post-apocalyptic battle for domination of the planet will be waged between cockroaches, gonococci and the flies imbedded in my fishing hat.

Anyway, I am almost ready to be off fishing. I have only to sling my hip boots over my shoulder and slip out the back door.

I'm more than half glad that it is night, because if a fellow angler spotted me in my fishing gear, he would guffaw cruelly. My outfit is pretty far removed from the sort of thing one sees on the covers of angling magazines. Take the hip boots slung over my shoulder, for example. I am aware that there have been technical breakthroughs regarding material, that one can now purchase hip boots that can withstand re-entry into the earth's atmosphere. My own are made of rubber. They are so thoroughly composed of rubber molecules that I can imagine Old Man Goodyear saying, "Hey, we can make not only automobile tires but fishin' pants as well!" And they have little circles of rubber running the length of them (concentrated around the knees, sure, but represented everywhere), which are themselves encircled by ridges of rubber cement. Many of these repairs were performed streamside, mostly by the Old Guy himself, who is nothing if not helpful. This means that the inside of my hip boots is clammy and damp, for not all, or even many, of the seals are perfect.

And what of my fishing rod itself, which I've forgotten about? I mean, I really forgot about it. I have to go back into the house (inspiring the moronic dog, who saw me leave a few seconds ago, to a bout of house-wakening yelping) to retrieve it. But now that I have it and am flinging it into the back seat of the car, isn't there something a little odd-looking about it? Well, indeed so. It, too, is old. Parts of it are older than others. The tip section is relatively recent, for example, while the butt was acquired long ago. In a couple of places the rod has little raised sections, like the clitellums on worms. These are evidence of Old Guy repair work, too (the raised sections formed by thread and nail polish), but these are much more trustworthy than the boot repairs.

I'll describe the reel to you as I drive up the Don Valley Parkway into the wilds of Scarborough. The good thing about driving at four o'clock in the morning is that the traffic is all right, even in Toronto. It will only take me about ten minutes to drive from downtown to the Old Guy's house in Scarborough, a journey that in rush hour might take days. Those of you in other places may not appreciate the relationship Scarborough has to downtown Toronto. Officially, of course, we have conglomerated into one big megacity, but Scarborough remains a satellite, a dark moon, a land of squat houses and high-rises, traversed every which way by armies of hydro towers. In short, it is not where one might expect to find an outdoorsman like my Old Guy.

Oh, we're turning on to Warden Avenue now, approaching Tower Drive, so I must do what I said I was going to do— describe my reel. Well, it is much smaller than many you've seen, and is largely covered by a big elastic band. I need the band to keep the line ravelled about the spool, because there is no bail. The bail is that piece of metal that covers the face of the reel and effects the catching and the retrieval of line. I don't have a bail, even though it sounds mighty useful, doesn't it?

Why don't I have one? Because I cut it off. On purpose.

My Old Guy made me do it.

We'll get to that in a bit. If you, dear reader, are confused and disoriented by my leaping narrative, it is only to give you some notion of my muddled faculties at four-thirty in the morning.

The Old Guy lives on a suburban crescent, his house sitting in the middle of the curve, right on the bulge, as it were. His house stands out from the rest. For one thing, there is a huge maple tree on the lawn; clinging to it are seven or eight huge silver cans, collecting sap. Few people do that in the suburbs, you know. But Gordon does many things that few suburbanites do. I remember he once telephoned the city officials to ask if he was allowed to pick off the squirrels on his lawn. "Well, I guess so," they allowed. "It's your property." So the Old Guy was out on his lawn, shooting varmints, which was no doubt an alarming sight for his neighbours.

For another thing, the Old Guy's driveway is usually occupied by homemade trailers and collapsible boats and Ski-Doos in various states of disrepair. The Ski-Doos are for ice fishing, which is one of the Old Guy's obsessions. Mind you, the Old Guy is hardly one for sitting in a little hut all day, staring into an iridescent opening in the ice floor. He has purchased a small plastic structure that can be hastily erected, but this is mostly in deference to his wife, Sheila. The Old Guy's conception of ice fishing is to tear around on his Ski-Doo, stopping occasionally to auger a quick hole, stick in the line, see what happens. He gives it a few moments and then he's roaring off to another spot. This is very arduous, it seems to me, although the Old Guy loves it. I'm sure he's trying to figure out some way of trolling out there on the floes, although so far it's eluded him, despite his manifest craftiness.

His car I have described in *Fishing With My Old Guy*, the huge multi-finned land yacht. In truth, the Old Guy has recently acquired a neat little off-roading suv, but I'm going to imagine the land yacht. There is a glow coming from within the cab—the interior light has been turned on—and as I walk up the driveway, carting my stuff, I can make out the silhouette of the Old Guy—Gordon, his name is—slumped over in the driver's seat. The most distinctive aspect of this silhouette is his fishing hat, which is of the sort worn by the cartoon character Andy Capp, although the Old Guy's hat seems to have exploded at several points, little tufts erupting from the material, perhaps created when Gordon had particularly good ideas.

I open the door on the passenger's side. The Old Guy is sitting with his hand wrapped around a coffee cup. The radio is going, broadcasting news and weather. The Old Guy is sound asleep.

"Hey," I say, and the Old Guy awakens with a start, although there is no groggy transition from slumber to alertness; he turns on the ignition, fires up the land yacht's engine and wishes me a good morning. I climb into the car and we head off, to the east of Toronto. It is but a few moments before we are on the superhighway. I suppose that's one of the reasons Gordon likes his little home in Scarborough; it is handy to the 401, the Parkway, the major thoroughfares that give Gordon access to all his fishing spots. And he has many, many fishing spots. I once asked why he didn't buy a cottage or a cabin somewhere, and that was the gist of his answer, that there were too many places that he liked to fish.

We are heading toward the Ganaraska River, near Port Hope, Ontario. Several of the places that Gordon likes to fish are on this river, and he has given them all names like The Picnic Grounds and Itsy-Bitsy. He believes that I know which are which, but I don't. All I know is that my favourite place to fish is the one where we turn left at a farm, drive across the farmer's field and down a muddy pathway to the river. This journey is particularly exciting in the early spring; Gordon will often stop the land yacht and stare at the "road" ahead, trying to judge its worthiness. After a few moments, Gordon will shrug and press his foot down on the accelerator. There is danger involved here; the land yacht could lose purchase and slide down into a deep gully, and I often imagine that the Old Guy gives those few moments over, not to a consideration of safety, but rather to a philosophical acceptance of death.

Oh, I should make some mention of the conversation we have during the drive, which takes perhaps an hour. A frequent topic of conversation is the activities of the club he formed years ago, the Scarborough Fly and Bait Casting Association. This is how

I met the Old Guy—I saw an ad in a newspaper suggesting I could be a much better fisherman than I was. Well, I knew that, because I was a lousy fisherman, but I was keen and I was youngish so one night I drove to a schoolhouse in Scarborough and watched Gordon demonstrate his casting abilities. I eagerly ponied up twenty-five dollars for the club dues. He stuck a fly rod in my hand and had me demonstrate my casting abilities. While I was doing so, the Old Guy snuck up behind me and pressed his knees into the back of mine, making me buckle and crouch. "That's the best position for any athletic activity," he informed me, and then he stood in front of me, mere inches away, preventing my forward cast from becoming too exaggerated. He took hold of my hand with both of his and kept my wrist in proximity to the cork butt. I was a poor fly-caster, I knew that, but I was a better fly-caster after a few minutes spent with the Old Guy. "That's good," he said, "we'll see you next week."

Again, I add shamelessly, much of our relationship is detailed in *Fishing With My Old Guy*. It has had its ups and downs, some which stemmed from the fact that the Old Guy was, for his professional life, an insurance salesman. Man, I own a lot of insurance. I've got so much insurance that I probably get a little bit of money when *you* die.

But that's neither here nor there—the Old Guy has retired now and applies all of his nonfishing energy to one goal: getting published. And that is mostly what we talk about on our trip to the Ganaraska River. "Have you sent anyone *Free Food 'n Fun?*" This is a book about, basically, consuming the wilderness, finding comestibles out in the wild. It's actually a splendid little piece of work, and I think I did send it to some publishing acquaintance of mine, who no doubt threw it on top of the slush pile or gave it to a subordinate so that he or she could throw it onto the slush pile. Anyway, I don't have an answer, and Gordon sighs and laments his lot and extracts from me a promise to do better.

We climb out of the car and make ready. This involves putting on our rubber waders—if you think mine are old, you should see Gordon's—and setting up our rods. When we are wearing chest waders, a difference comes to light—namely, I would cinch a belt about the belly whilst Gordon chooses not to. This has to do—not to be too dramatic about it—with how we choose to battle death, death coming as a tumble into fast-moving water. I say that the belt will keep water *out* of the waders, Gordon believes a belt would keep it *in*. I bring this up, not because either hypothesis is necessarily correct (one wouldn't want to test them), but to illustrate that I don't necessarily do everything he tells me to. This has been a slight source of friction during our relationship, because Gordon pretty much demands total obedience from his acolytes. And I resist certain of his methods. One I resisted for a long time—although I eventually relented—was chopping the bail off my reel.

I'll return to the riverside so that I might give a graphic illustration of what I'm talking about. I fix the two parts of my rod together (some might think this a shortish rod, a mere 5 feet from butt to tip), and then I take the elastic band from the reel. Immediately the monofilament overflows and spills out onto the ground. Why? Because there is nothing—like a goddam *bail*, for example—to prevent it from doing so. Once I thread the line through the guides and tie a number 3 Mepps to the end, it becomes more tractable and I can hook the line under a little knob—the remnants of the bail—to maintain tension. But many might wonder why I would seemingly cause myself grief.

Well, I will now explain that the Old Guy and I are about to fish in a rather uncommon manner. It is not the sedentary, bucolic method of trout fishing, sitting on a bank and dangling a worm and a bobber. Neither is it the rarefied pursuit of well-kitted nimrods, standing in the stream and gently lofting little flies into distant pools. What Gordon and I are going to do this morning is, well, rather strenuous small-stream trout fishing in heavy cover. Gordon is picking his way down toward the river now, eager to say hello to the water.

He approaches stealthily (he has great respect for the quarry and treats them as though they were skittish as fawns) and settles on one knee a few feet from the bank. There is tall grass (some sort of vegetation, anyway; I'm not half the naturalist I should be), which he carefully parts with the side of his hand. In the river ahead, two trees have fallen, and at the far side the trees come together to form a V. That V is clearly occupied by an intermingling of branches contributed by both fallen trees.

That V is surely where a trout lives.

Gordon raises his rod, the seat of the reel sitting between his second and third fingers. With his index finger, he carefully lifts the line from its resting place on the bail remnant. He lets out line, allowing the Mepps to dangle a foot or so from the tip. Then, with a rhythmic precision worthy of an orchestral conductor, he moves the rod tip first down, then up, then down once more, and the line shoots out.

Now, despite the fact that the Old Guy's casting skills have earned him numerous national and international awards, I am going to write of something that happens, albeit infrequently—an imperfect cast. In this case, Gordon knows the instant after he's released the line that it is going to fall short of the crotch of the V. The lure is destined to splash down short of its target and spook the fish sitting in the V, so Gordon slams his index finger onto the spool, stopping the line, and jerks his hand backward. The lure comes screaming back—right toward my face—but I manage to dodge out of the way.

This is the main advantage of bail removal. The index finger can get onto the spool immediately. With your more common spinning reel, precious instants are used up by cranking the handle (this is how the bail is engaged). So, for example, when the Old Guy makes his next cast—which is perfect—his finger is on the line even before the lure touches water. He is in control from that magical first moment, working the lure, making it twitch and flutter, convincing the ever-wary trout that a bug has landed in the water and needs to be eaten.

A fish is taken, a nice little rainbow, a "bow" in the parlance of this book. The Old Guy deals with the thing streamside, dispatching it, cleaning it, shrouding it with watercress in his creel.

We move on to the next spot. Again, fallen trees have created a wonderful little lair for some fine fish. This hole is protected, screened by many trees that have yet to fall.

"Okay, Kew," says the Old Guy, who calls me that, "Q," because over the years there has been confusion with other Pauls. "Okay, Kew," he says, "your shot."

"No, no, Gordon, you go ahead." I am not being nice, I am being testy and passively aggressive, because the cast looks impossible.

"Come on," he says. "Pendulum cast should work."

Again I demur, but there is no demurral before the Old Guy's determination. "Come on," Gordon snaps, "we've got a lot of river to get to."

I sigh and approach the river. I assume a half-crouch, the best position for any athletic activity. With my index finger I lift the line and let it drop. I allow it to drop until the lure would just about reach the reel. Then I start a slow swinging, and at a moment that is nearly coincident with the lure being farthest away, I execute the little conductor move with the rod tip: up/down/up. Out shoots line. This method of casting allows me to scoot under all the overhanging branches, you see. And then my index finger lights upon the spool once more, stopping line, and it drops and—well hey, I'm writing this introduction—the lure drops sweetly into trout territory.

Nothing happens.

"Hmmm," shrugs the Old Guy. "Too bad. That was a nice cast."

Now, I wouldn't want you, dear reader, to be searching for subtext and hidden agenda here. I don't want you to think that perhaps the Old Guy knew full well there was no trout there, perhaps had even evicted the fishy himself, and was simply making me perform a very hard cast for purposes of mischief or vexation. After all, I can imagine you thinking, didn't you say dealing with a guy was a challenge? Well, he is a challenge, because this sort of thing happens all morning long. We will arrive at a spot and Gordon will appraise it and he'll point out an undercut that lies beyond a submerged log and is protected by branches and, I don't know, electromagnetic fields, and this spot can only be cast to whilst dangling upside down from a slick and slippery bower, and the Old Guy will say, "Okay, Kew. Your shot."

Over the course of the morning, I make the shots. Some are dismal failures and result in the loss of terminal tackle, either in the trees above the river or between the rocks in its bed. Some casts are successful but receive no reward. But I do manage to catch two fish.

That's how the Old Guy challenges you. He challenges you to be the best fisherman you can be. Let's face it, if I were fishing the river alone, I would have walked by most of those fishing holes, casting only to the easily accessible homes of tiddlers, which is what the Old Guy and I call fishies of a few inches.

Mind you, he also challenges one by being a bit of a pain in the butt. Once he elects a direction—getting one of his manuscripts published, say—the Old Guy gets up a head of steam and storms away. He is a good writer, as you shall see, but often seems to judge his output according to the length of time it took to create. He is therefore liable to say, of a two-hundred-page effort, "God, Kew, this is a good one, it only took me three weeks to write!" Some of his subjects are a little too particular for mass publication. His book about the Ganaraska River, as delightful as it is, will find its largest market within driving distance of that river. His book *Fishing With Paul Quarrington by His Old Guy* will find its largest market within, well, hey I've already read the manuscript. So it was suggested to Gordon, by myself and by various intrigued parties, that he set down *everything* he knows. The Old Guy took a few seconds to decide that this sounded like a good idea, and he roared off and set to work on his little computer. He called a little while later to say that he was about halfway through. I advised him to slow down a little, and he agreed that this sounded like a good idea. A little while later he phoned to say that he'd finished the book. "I'll send it right over for you to read."

When the package arrived, I realized that I was to be midwife to the published work and there would be no getting out of that. Another challenge from Gordon.

The good news was, he'd done it! The Old Guy had put down everything he knew, and now everyone could share this knowledge without risking death (death in the form, for instance, of plummeting off a mucky cliffside trapped inside an old land yacht). I sent it off to the Publisher. I know many publishers, but only one I refer to with the capital P. You may have met the Publisher in another, earlier work of mine, *The Boy on the Back of the Turtle*. He's a very good Publisher, because when you suggest things like, "I want to go to the Galápagos Islands with my seven-year-old daughter and seventy-year-old father" (such is indeed the premise of "Turtle Boy"), the Publisher nods and allows as it's a good idea. He also is a keen angler. The Publisher and I have fished many times, most notably from a little bucking driftboat piloted by a legendary guide named Joe Seychelles. But I'm getting ahead of myself and also shamelessly promoting a recent work of mine, a collection of fishing writing, including an account of a shoot down B.C.'s Cowichan River, entitled "My Side of the River," to be published by the Publisher, of course.

But getting back to the Old Guy's book, I made the following suggestion to the Publisher. "Perhaps I could add my own voice to Gordon's, as a kind of editorial commentary." The Publisher, being who he is, thought that sounded like a grand idea. You got to love the guy.

So that is how we shall proceed, dear reader. You hold in your hands a book entitled *Fishing for Brookies, Browns & Bows*, being the collected wisdom of master angler Gordon Deval, with commentary by acolyte and friend Paul Quarrington.

Let's go.

Prologue

. . . .

$\mathcal{I}$ have spent more than sixty years fishing for and refining techniques for catching those beautiful finny fellows called trout. Ever since I was seven years old and began fishing for brookies in a tiny creek, I have been pursuing that Holy Grail of all fishes, the World Record Brook Trout.

I owe much of my passion for trout fishing to my Uncle Bob, who introduced me to that first trout stream and consequently to my first trout, a 6-inch jewel of a brookie. I also have to blame another gentleman no longer with us, Dave Reddick (who was president of the Toronto Anglers and Hunters Association in the forties and was an excellent tournament caster and fly-fisherman), for contributing to my devotion to the sport. It was he whom I surreptitiously followed about on the Toronto Islands' lagoons, marvelling at the beauty and grace of his fly-casting prowess, until, finally spotting me behind him, he convinced me that I should learn how to fly-fish and ultimately become a tournament caster myself.

During my youth, several other well-known anglers and tournament fly- and bait-casters helped shape my interests in the more technical aspects of angling: Carl Atwood (author

Margaret Atwood's father), who as a respected entomologist and superb fly-tier taught me the basics of that rewarding pastime; Jack Sutton, whose brain I picked on many an occasion in matters dealing with trout fishing; Frank Kortright, president of the old Toronto Anglers and Hunters Association (where I earned my stripes as a tournament caster); Claude Owens, who gave me the gift of appreciation for bamboo and its wonderful properties when teaching me how to make my first split-cane fly rod; Myron Gregory, who spent hours answering the questions I mailed him with lengthy written explanations of fly-line construction and design; and last, Lee Wulff, whose wonderful talks and film presentations on salmon and brook trout fishing inspired me to attempt to follow in his path.

> Q: *Margaret Atwood once told me that she has trout flies that she and her father tied together. I mention that, not to impress you with my friendship with Ms. Atwood—Peggy, we call her—but rather to name-drop rather shamelessly.*

As Paul Quarrington explained in his wonderful little book *Fishing With My Old Guy*, everyone requires one or more Old Guys (men of experience who can pass that experience on to others) if they expect to acquire even a semblance of expertise in pretty well any sporting activity. All those wonderful gentlemen mentioned in the preceding paragraph were the Old Guys who helped shape my destiny, such as it is, in the angling world.

"But why fish just for trout?" I am often asked. First there is the aesthetics. Unlike other types of fishing, most trout fishing requires time to be spent in pristine surroundings—clear, unpolluted water, such as spring-fed lakes, bubbling ice-cold headwater brooks or photogenic northern streams, replete with rapids and waterfalls.

Then there is the beauty of the fish themselves. I am always amazed by the diversity of coloration to be admired on brookies, browns and bows, unlike that of their distant, fishy relatives, bass, pickerel, pike and so on. The resplendent hues and esoteric markings of brookies, for example, are almost impossible for even the best of taxidermists to duplicate. Yet, non-trout fishermen looking at the trout on the walls in my home invariably ask, "Are they really that colourful?"

A large part of the allure of trout fishing for me is the various skills that are required to be a complete trout angler. The spinoffs using these skills are so varied that many folks decide to specialize in one of them and seldom actually wet a line in search of trout. These skills include knowledge of where in the lake or stream to present their offerings, fly-tying, rod building, competitive casting, habitat study and the art of formulating credible fish stories.

Also, like track-and-field athletes, always striving to cut precious seconds or add inches and feet to their results, some trout fishermen are always attempting personal bests of their own or chasing records such as Dr. Cook's almost century-old 14½-pound brook trout record.

Lastly, trout can be prepared for the table in a number of delightful ways. Far surpassing the usual frying pan full of bass fillets, trout lend themselves to everything from simple gravlax or sushi to dilled and grilled steaks, steamed or baked recipes and so on. The variety of ways you can prepare trout is limited only by your imagination.

Although I would rather catch trout on flies that I have made myself, I am on occasion not averse to using spinners, wobblers, plugs, worms, minnows, crawfish, frogs, grubs, grasshoppers, roe, sponge or almost anything else as bait. Nevertheless, I do draw the line at spears, dynamite caps, nets or set lines (baited rigs tied to sealed and floating plastic bottles or over-hanging branches). Amusingly, my using tackle other than fly-fishing equipment draws disdain from certain quarters, folks who fancy themselves as superior anglers because they only use artificial flies to hunt down their quarry.

I learned long ago, however, that many of these "fishermen" are really not true anglers. They merely talk the good talk, rarely ever wetting a line themselves, their angling hours consisting of reading fishing magazines or books and watching awful fishing shows on television. Some of them do practise fly-tying, which they seem to believe gives them the right to put down all other forms of fishing.

> Q: *Gordon is one of those fellows, I believe, who doesn't feel quite right unless he's got a feud or two ongoing. The Old Guy has chosen this book to start mixing it up with the people I referred to in my introduction as "well-kitted nimrods." People who buy their fishing tackle at Abercrombie and Fitch. People with space-age hip waders. I'm not sure how many of these people Gordon has actually encountered (they typically don't venture into the kind of deep cover that Gordon favours), but I know he hates the idea of them. He hates snobbery; he hates anything that isn't democratic. That is why, despite an assertion he is going to make, he is no great respecter of Private Property notices. Anyway, we shall see more of this anti-nimrod attitude anon.*

Fishing for Brookies, Browns & Bows will delve into all aspects of fishing for these species, the most sought after, the crème de la crème in the world of trout, even though there are a number of dissimilar members of the trout and char families, such as lake trout, cutthroat, Dolly Varden and other lesser-known species and subspecies.

> Q: *You know, that sentence I really should do something with. The point is, we're going to be discussing the Big Three.*

Although there certainly are similarities between brook, brown and rainbow trout, there are a number of differences. Most notable, perhaps, are the differences in size. Angling for brookies in small streams and tiny brooks seldom produces catches of fish exceeding a foot in length, with the norm averaging between 6 and 9 inches.

Larger fish are found in larger waters, such as ponds and lakes; some may be in excess of 3 or 4 pounds. A few of these lakes actually contain these gorgeous fish weighing more than 7 or 8 pounds, while the largest specimens of brook trout, weighing as much as 9 or 10 pounds, come from the white-water rivers of the Far North.

Brookies are the most spectacularly coloured of the three, in contrasting shades of scarlet, black and ivory, their flanks bedecked with ivory spots interspersed with brilliant red dots, each surrounded by iridescent cobalt-blue halos. The coloration of a brook trout's flesh ranges from pink to a deep orange-red.

These fish can be moody and difficult to engage in large bodies of water but are normally quite receptive to a variety of enticements in streams and lakes. Of the three fish, brookies prefer the coldest waters and will not survive for long in water above 65°F.

Brown trout, originally a European import, are occasionally found in lakes and impoundments where they may have been stocked, but they are most often fished for in rivers and streams. Like brookies, they prefer colder waters, but they can survive quite nicely in water temperatures as high as 70°F. Because of extensive stocking, browns can be found virtually all over North America. Although not in the same league as brookies, they, too, often have beautiful, occasionally intense coloration, ranging from silver to golden or brownish hues, with brown and red spots. The size and number of spots can vary enormously in both brookies and browns.

Brown trout are usually considered the most popular quarry for fly-fishermen, although a large part of a brown's diet often consists of many creatures other than insect life. Most browns caught in streams range from 9 to 15 inches in length, but many waters produce much larger specimens. Brown trout are known to exceed 20 pounds in the Great Lakes and in some western waters and impoundments in the Midwest. Both brookies and browns will in some areas migrate from their home rivers and streams to lakes and even coastal salt waters, where they may reach phenomenal size.

Although they do not provide the gastronomic fare for which brookies are famous, browns can offer a delightful repast if caught from cold, spring-fed streams. Most, however, are released by anglers to fight another day.

Found almost everywhere, bows are an entirely different kettle of fish. There is now such a tremendous diversity of rainbow trout and its cousin, and perhaps predecessor, Kamloops trout, that coloration ranges from a silvery-blue and olive, with black fleck marks, to a silvery-greenish colour with a slash of red extending from the gill covers to the tail, as well as black flecking—and everything in between. Originally located in the lakes (Kamloops trout) and rivers of the West Coast, as far north as Alaska, these powerful fighters have been stocked and altered by biologists so many times in so many different waters that now there seems to be tremendous variety in the entire makeup of the fish.

Because they are the easiest of the three trout to locate in most areas, bows are extremely popular with trout fishermen. They are the most spectacular fighter of the three, often performing acrobatic cartwheels and making powerful dashes away from the angler one moment, then racing towards their adversary the next.

Bows are found in streams, ponds, lakes and oceans. In many areas, they migrate from the sea and lakes into the streams and rivers to spawn, at which time they are referred to as steelhead trout, or steelheads. Rainbow trout up to 5 or 6 pounds provide fine table fare, whereas larger specimens should be reserved for the smoker. Rainbows residing all year in streams seldom grow larger than a few pounds, but migratory fish in lakes and large bodies of water, like browns, can tip the scales in excess of 25 pounds.

Fishermen use everything from lowly pea-sized pieces of sponge, kernels of corn or dew worms to spinners, spoons, roe bags, flies, plugs and live bait to catch rainbow trout. Bows are the easiest of the three trout to raise in hatcheries—thus the tremendous growth in their popularity with fishermen everywhere, private water or otherwise.

Whether I am fishing for brookies, browns or bows, the equipment carried on my person varies little, depending on the season or if I am fly-fishing. One constant—except for ice-fishing excursions, when I dress in thermal underwear and down clothing and am prepared for anything the elements can throw at me—is my trusty fishing vest. Only the loss of my lucky old fishing hat would hurt more than losing my twenty-year-old vest with its myriad pockets, many of which have still to be discovered. I recently learned that some of the larger pockets on this thing actually have secondary, smaller pockets within them. Most trout fishermen wear fishing vests of one kind or another, some containing potentially lifesaving inflatable features, others with detachable nylon mesh creels. The creel is the main reason I wear the vest, although the pockets do come in handy for the comparatively insignificant assortment of gear that I carry on the stream.

Whereas most fishermen seem to enjoy stuffing every pocket in their fishing vest with some gadget or another, the list of contents in my old vest has been refined to absolute minimal necessities. Those other fishermen have never been able to explain to me the logic behind their stuffed pockets. The mentality seems to be that all those pockets are there for a reason, so accordingly, why not fill them up? I learned over fifty years ago that on a 3-or-4-mile hike through the bush, one's vest can become quite a load on the back and shoulders if the pockets are laden with unnecessary tackle and potpourri.

A sampling of the contents in my vest would reveal three or four lures in a small cough-drop box, a 35mm film canister containing several Despair flies, leader tippet material, camera, spare film, folding cup, sandwich, Muskol insect repellent, head net compressed into a pill tube, assorted zip-lock plastic bags, elastics, 10 feet of 50-pound test nylon cord, nail clippers, hemostat, a few Band-Aids and perhaps the most valuable item, a flattened, partial roll of toilet paper sealed in a zip-lock bag.

When fishing with spinning tackle, I might carry a spare spool for my reel, loaded with 6-pound test monofilament, and when fly-fishing, a spare spool for the fly reel with either a floating or sinking line, the opposite of whichever is on the reel. I have actually seen fishermen, miles upstream, carrying large tackle boxes, stuffed with hundreds of lures and other paraphernalia, through cedar bush and swamps.

Another essential item always on my person, but never in my vest, is an old Swiss Army knife, the one with all the extra tools built into it. That is basically all I require, along with my tackle, boots and vest, to do battle in pursuit of my passion, fishing for brookies, browns and bows.

Brook Trout

CHAPTER ONE

The Aristocratic Brookie

. . . .

Resplendent in their lavishly coloured regal coats, brookies must be considered the aristocrats of the trout world. *Salvelinus fontinalis*, speckled trout, specks, brook trout, brookies, Quebec reds, squaretails—whatever name you apply to this beautiful fish, you should know that although it is generally categorized as a trout, technically it is a char. The confusion occurs because the fish was called a trout for many years before researchers discovered it was a char, and the name has stuck. Brook trout are found predominantly in eastern Canada and the northeastern United States, with some light distribution in British Columbia, Alberta and eastern Manitoba.

How to Find Brook Trout Waters
. . . .

Specks can be found in brooks as tiny as a foot or so across and only a few inches deep, as well as in larger streams, rivers, ponds and, of course, small and occasionally large lakes. The main requisites for an ecosystem capable of supporting specks are pollution-free water of a reasonably consistent temperature, normally maintained by cold, free-flowing freshwater springs; enough cover to provide shelter and shade; a sandy or gravelly streambed; and a natural food supply, such as insect life, minnows or crawfish.

Few large ponds and lakes are capable of maintaining a natural stock of brookies through the fish's own spawning efforts. Even though the brookies do not seem to realize it, their spawning actions all go for naught, since the fertilized eggs require gravel, or at least sand and small stones, and running water to prevent them from becoming covered with silt before they reach maturity.

Those lakes with cold, free-flowing streams or rivers entering them are the only exceptions, certainly in the warmer, more southerly regions of Canada. Many of the lake and river systems in the far northern areas—such as Manitoba's God's River and the Nipigon, Winisk and Albany watersheds in northern Ontario, as well as most of the rivers of northern Quebec and Labrador—contain all the requirements for the maintenance of superlative brook trout stocks and fine fishing.

In southern Ontario, numerous private ponds, such as those at the famous Caledon and Glen Major Clubs, contain brookies that were stocked as fingerlings or yearlings, but comparatively few fishermen are financially fortunate enough to be able to share in this rather easy fishing pastime. There are, however, other ponds maintained by various conservation authorities that also support brookies and that are available to anybody willing to pay what is usually a nominal sum for the privilege.

Many of these commercial and Natural Resources ponds are stocked with rainbow trout, but not brookies, because bows generally mature faster and are less susceptible to fluctuations in water temperature than are brook trout. They are fine places to take children for their first trout-fishing trips, as the youngsters can be reasonably assured of seeing and catching a few trout without the difficulties they would face if deposited on a trout stream or brook in the middle of the bush, as I was as a child. There were no conservation areas back then.

Although the great waters of the far reaches of the provinces contain the biggest brookies, which draw my fishing buddies and me to the North in search of the proverbial pot o' gold at least once a year, superlative fishing for brook trout can often be found as well in lakes only a couple of hours from the big southern cities, also courtesy of the Natural Resources Ministries and their various stocking and licensing programs. Many fishermen are not aware that brookies can be located in waters other than small creeks and streams and that these fish can grow to be even larger than the more popular and common smallmouth bass with which they are probably most familiar.

> Q: *Brookies are everywhere! Gordon, quite shrewdly, is always asking the Ministry of Natural Resources where the various stocking programs are taking place. Such things are not secret, after all, and pose no threat to national security. So they tell him and give him maps, and the Old Guy goes and scouts them out. There can be very pleasant surprises. One target lake was about a mile from my in-laws' home.*

Fishing these speckled trout lakes, stocked or otherwise, calls for a different set of criteria than does angling in streams and brooks. In springtime, immediately after the ice disappears, excellent fishing can be had in some of these waters as the trout work the inshore waters, gorging on the minnows attracted to the runoff from the melting snow in the bush. The shiners and chubs congregate in schools searching for their own food and, in turn, attract the hungry brookies.

Within a week or so of ice-out, the trout seem to disappear, but they are just reluctant to strike at anything for a few weeks because they are sated. When the black flies and mosquitoes make their annual unpleasant return, however, the brookies can once again be taken, although now in slightly deeper water than at ice-out time.

Eventually, as the surface water warms, the lake stratifies into layers. Feeding fish normally occupy the middle (thermocline) layer. Brook trout favour water temperatures from 52° to 54°F, which are most often located in the middle of the thermocline. In small to midsized lakes, that depth would normally be between 7 and 15 feet until midsummer, when, as the waters warm, the ideal temperatures are several feet deeper.

These guidelines are applicable to most lakes containing brookies, but there are exceptions. During a mayfly hatch, the brookies will forsake the cool depths to feed on mayfly nymphs wiggling just beneath the surface, as well as on adults struggling out of their cases and drying their wings on top of the water after they have emerged.

I have taken brookies under these conditions that had absolutely gorged on the nymphs. They contained perhaps hundreds of nymphs in their stomachs, and most were still alive when the trout were cleaned. I have even cleaned brookies the day after they were caught and discovered live mayfly larvae in the stomachs; I gave them a light rinse and kept them in a glass of water on the windowsill for a few days. As a trout fisherman and fly-tier, I found them fascinating to observe.

Q: These autopsies and experiments are not really as fascinating as all that, but they give a clue to the Old Guy's intensely curious mindset. There is a practical reason for examining the contents of a fish's tummy — see what it's been eating and then offer its schoolmates a facsimile

of same—but I have seen Gordon stare at his besmirched
thumbnail (he will use his thumbnail as a sort of stream-
side specimen slide) for many long moments, fascinated by
any evidence of the intricate workings of life.

I find it almost impossible to catch these trout by attempting to match their winged and wiggling quarry with my fly-
tying efforts, but offering them something entirely different,
such as a large wobbler or Flatfish, will occasionally persuade
them to sample my lure. Large minnows can also be surpris-
ingly effective, as can a trolled spinner or gang troll with a fat
dew worm dangling enticingly behind.

In general, I concentrate on the lower reaches of the thermocline during the summer. During the first hour of daylight
in the morning and the last in the evening, however, some
trout in some lakes will work the surface near shoals.

As a youngster I first fished for brookies in small streams,
and today most of my brook trout fishing hours are still spent
in streams. An insignificant trickle may hold some of the most
beautiful brook trout imaginable. If the required food, shelter,
water quality and temperature are in place and the brookies either are native to the brook or have luckily found their way
into these minuscule flows from larger bodies of water, they
will thrive and provide fine sport—and dining potential.

How to Find Brookies

But how do you find these prized locations? I am always amazed
at the number of ponds and small lakes—literally in the hundreds—that are easily visible from the air as one flies into the
Toronto airport. Most appear to be well within an hour's drive of
the city.

Many of these waters are simply decorative additions to expensively landscaped properties or just swampy duck ponds, but with a little research I have learned that a great many are actually spring-fed trout ponds. If you live in the Toronto area, you are in one of the easiest places to begin a search for your own little brook trout Shangri-La.

Wherever there is one of these ponds already stocked with brookies, either freshwater springs support the pond or it is fed by a spring-fed brook. But it also must have an outlet. Although rainbow trout do not require the cold influx of fresh water that brook trout do, ponds with a brookie population will always have an outflow, usually controlled by a dam.

Find one of these ponds and the resultant brook flowing from it, and you will probably also find your own brook trout stream. Where these ponds are normally established, many springs feed not just the main body of water but also any watershed that has resulted from the building of the pond, including all the creeks, streams and brooks in the area. A little research and poking around is all it takes to discover one of these sites, where you can spend a pleasurable hour or two when you can escape your chores.

If you want to avoid driving around the boondocks looking for these places, up-to-date topographical maps will show you precisely where these hot spots can be found. They often show even the tiniest trickles of water near the ponds.

A few polite inquiries to the property owners will usually result in the information you really want—what kind of trout do they have in their pond, and would they allow you to fish there? One approach I have used successfully several times after introducing myself, but before posing these questions, is to say, "I am writing a magazine article on trout ponds and trying to collect as much information as possible."

Of course, you must immediately reassure the party that you have no intention of attempting to fish their pond. If they should ask what publication you are attached to, simply state that you are independent and intend to submit the finished article to several magazines, such as *Harrowsmith* or whatever. It is also advantageous to have a 35mm camera hanging on your chest to give you a little more credibility.

> Q: *Aha! The old "I'm a journalist" scam. I've worked the "I'm a journalist" scam many times and found it to be not as effective as Gordon might be implying. And hey, I'm a journalist! I find that in this, as in life, honesty is the best policy.*

As I mentioned before, most often a firm yet polite approach will provide you with all the information you require—and sometimes even more. I have actually been invited to try my hand fishing on several such ponds. Nevertheless, one must be prepared for a rather curt and negative response. The truth is, I have been told on more than one or two occasions, "Now just get the hell off my property!"

> Q: *More than one or two occasions a day, more like. As I've said before, it rankles the Old Guy on a very profound level that people should be allowed to own the land and control the places where he wants to fish. The fish heed no such jurisdictions, so why should he? He's a proud poacher, and I have been with him on more than one or two of the one or two such occasions he mentions. Gordon turns and goes quietly, although always with a queer half-smile on his face, one that seems to sing like a schoolboy, "I know something you don't know . . ."*
>
> *And oh, yeah—there's usually dogs involved.*

The Importance of Habitat

. . . .

Successful fishing for specks in these tiny headwater areas does require a different approach from fishing in larger rivers, ponds or lakes. Some of the brooks that I enjoy wetting a line in are so small that you can easily stand with a foot on each side of the creek while trying to find a hole in the cover in which to present your lure.

There is an area near the town of Uxbridge, about a forty-minute drive from where I live, with a number of private spring-fed ponds as well as two larger ponds within the town limits. The town ponds are stocked periodically with rainbow and brook trout and, on the odd occasion, a few good-size browns.

There are, however, a great number of brooks, streams, creeks and just plain trickles in this spring-rich area that support a semi-permanent population of brookies. Because these minuscule flows are so consistently cold (averaging about 48°F), the resident trout are gorgeously coloured specimens with a rich, orange hue to their flesh and are absolutely delectable table fare.

One of my favourite memories goes back almost fifty years to the day I decided to drive up to Uxbridge and spend an hour or two fishing in one of the brooks below the town pond. As it turned out, I was not the only one who woke up that day with the idea of chasing down a few brookies to bring home for supper.

For some reason or other, the old Ford parked on the side of the gravel road failed to catch my attention. Slipping on my hip boots a little way down the road from where I had parked my car, I decided to avoid the more heavily fished area, where the creek crossed beneath the road, and to access it instead a hundred yards downstream. Usually the trails disappear rather quickly beyond the point of easiest access.

A few yards into the bush, I could hear the brook gurgling seductively, inviting me forward through a dense growth of 6-foot-tall ostrich ferns. Suddenly I spotted a fisherman sitting by the edge of the creek.

It was my mother.

Comfortably ensconced in a bend of the huge curling root of a cedar tree, she held a paperback book in one hand, her fishing rod in the other, while her line simply disappeared through the grassy blanket topping the little brook. Mom was so engrossed in her book, probably a Harlequin Romance novel, that she was completely unaware of both her son's presence and the gentle twitching of her rod tip.

Trying not to unduly alarm her, I gently said, "Mother, I think you've got one on. Using worms, eh?"

Without batting an eye she replied, "Of course I'm using worms. How else can you fish here? Oh! Oh! Oh! It's you, Gordon! How did you know I was here?"

I explained that I hadn't known that she was fishing there—or even realized that she knew that there *was* fishing there—while she reeled in a plump 8-incher, efficiently dispatching it before threading a fresh dew worm onto her hook.

I have included this little anecdote not to show that my mom enjoyed trout fishing but to illustrate that if the water and habitat are suitable, brookies can be found in the most unpretentious of locales, even where the waters, almost invisible beneath the grasses, can only be heard. Like many others in that area, the brook disappears completely underground every few feet, only to pop up a little farther on in the bush.

The Search for "Real Brookies"
. . . .

During my thirteen-year tenure as a commercial traveller for a sporting goods firm, I had ample opportunity to investigate pretty well every stream, brook and river in my territory, searching for brook trout water. Even now, forty years later, there are hundreds of these relatively undiscovered places that can provide fine trout fishing.

I remember calling on a client in eastern Ontario, prepared to give him a couple of fat brookies that I had taken earlier from a stream that the highway crossed a half-mile down the road from his store. Much to my chagrin—although the brace of fine fish was politely accepted—he said, "Thanks, they're nice, Gord. I'll probably have 'em for breakfast tomorrow, but next time you know you're coming up this way, call me a day or so ahead of time and I'll show you some *real brookies!*"

I made a point of returning a few weeks later, much sooner than usual, and learned that he was true to his word. Ray Clemow, the gentleman who owned the little tackle shop, seemed pleased that I had taken him up on his offer to join him in finding some "real brookies."

"I'm glad you called ahead of time, Gord," he said, "because the pickerel season just opened and we're busier than hell up here right now."

Before I could interject a "Maybe we'd better leave it for another time," Ray said, "I'll see if I can get somebody to mind the shop for a few hours when you arrive tomorrow."

In fishing and tourist country, most bait and tackle shops have to be open for business early in the day and seldom close before eleven in the evening. Ordinarily, Ray's was no exception. When I showed up at his store a little after eight the following morning, however, he greeted me warmly (amazing what a gift of a brace of trout can do for a person), then announced that he was about to lock the door and, as soon as he finished tending to the few customers in the shop, we would be off.

"I couldn't find anybody who was free to come in and look after the store," he announced. "But don't worry, we'll only be gone for a couple of hours."

A short while later, with his faded, old GONE FISHIN' sign prominently displayed on the front door and "Be back in a couple of hours" written on a store receipt and taped to the bottom of the sign, we piled into Ray's Jeep and headed out to do battle with his "real brookies."

No more than twenty minutes later we were bouncing down an old logging road; then, abruptly leaving the "security" of the logging road, we made a sharp turn and cautiously wended our way through bumper-high grass and weeds, which, Ray assured me, was a trail. A trail to an abandoned gold mine, as a matter of fact. Eventually, with the Jeep mired in mud almost up to its doors, Ray chose discretion over valour, shut down the labouring engine and announced: "That's close enough, dammit! You don't mind walking a bit, do you?"

"No, not at all, Ray," I replied. Some of the streams that I fish close to home can keep me going for a couple of concession roads or more. I once wore a pedometer to check out a couple of my favourite waters. One day, doing Pefferlaw Creek, I recorded 12 miles on the gadget.

"Here, you'll need this," he said, casually tossing me an ancient, telescopic steel fishing rod. It was older than I, and considerably rustier. "It's the same as mine," he continued. "It's the only way that you can fish here, Gord. The stream's not very big, and there's bush and grass hanging over it everywhere."

"We just hook a dewy on," he explained, "then stick the rod through a hole between the bushes, push it out until the tip is above where you want to fish, then lower the bait into the creek. I'll show you in a moment or two."

I wanted to tell him that most of the trout streams I fish fitted his description of the one to which we were about to give a boo but decided it might sound a little smart-ass, so I left it alone. Not wishing to be rude to my host, I tagged along behind him with the telescopic pole visible in one hand, my ultralight spinning rod surreptitiously held in the other. A number 1 Silver Vibrax spinner was fastened to the 6-pound monofilament line.

With his finger on his pursed lips, Ray signalled that we were almost at the stream and should be quiet. Although I could hear the steam gurgling ahead of us, I certainly could not see it and had to agree that it would indeed be difficult to fish in the manner that I prefer, casting. But I was determined to illustrate to Ray that although it might be easier to fish with worms under these circumstances, an artificial lure can also do the trick if cast and fished accordingly.

I watched as Ray squatted low before feeding his 15-foot telescopic fishing rod out to its full length over the bushes. He looked back to see if I was paying attention before lowering his bait into what I guessed was water, then instantly yelped, "There's one!"

Sounds of frenzied splashing as the long pole was manoeuvred so that it could be shortened while the line was reeled in also suggested that a furious trout had engulfed the fat dew worm. When the line had achieved sufficient clearance, Ray raised the rod, brought it back over his shoulder, lifted a truly magnificent "real brookie" over his head and unceremoniously deposited it at my feet.

"All right, Ray!" I congratulated him. "It's a beauty, at least seventeen inches. You weren't kidding about your 'real brookies.'"

"Why don't you try the next hole?" he suggested. "That is, if you can find it through the scrub. The worms are in that can on the stump over there. Help yourself."

Chuckling, I thanked him, then said, "I hope you don't mind, Ray, but I'd really rather give this thing a try first. Okay?"

He said nothing but looked disappointed as I crept forward a few feet, then poked my way through the scrub until I could see a place that offered me a shot at the creek with the spinner. The spot was covered with long grass, however, which extended over the water from both banks.

No matter, I thought. If I can get away with fishing 2-foot-wide brooks near home, it should be even easier here with a stream that seems to be about 8 feet wide.

It worked as it was supposed to. The lure landed on what appeared to be the sparsest grass cover in the area, and a gentle jiggle of the rod tip helped it to break clear and strike the water. More frenetic splashing ensued as another "real brookie" nailed the little silver spinner, seemingly before the blade made its initial revolution. We caught four or five more beautiful brookies, all 2- to 3-pounders, when Ray, who was already impressed that his stream could be successfully fished with lures after all, announced, "Well, I hate to say it, but I've really got to get my ass back to the shop now, Gordon. I didn't think you could do it with that thing, but it looks like we each caught three—so I guess you don't really need worms to fish here after all.

"How do you like my little stream and its tenants?"

"Damned interesting fishing, Ray," I replied with a chuckle. "But I don't think I'll be dropping off any more brookies for your breakfast for a while."

I added, "I can see that you wouldn't have to hit this place very often to keep enough of your own trout in the freezer for a feed now and then. Like you said, these really are real brookies.

"Now what did you say the name of this creek is?"

Q: *That's fishing Old Guy style, for sure. I really think more people should do it, although preferably not on the same creeks as Gordon and I.*

CHAPTER TWO

Fishing for Brookies with Live Bait

. . . .

On days when the trout appear to be afflicted with a severe case of lockjaw and no fly or lure seems able to attract them from deep cover, a lively dew worm carefully weighted and drifted deeply into their living room can prove to be irresistible, even to a sullen brook trout in hiding. If you have promised your spouse that you will be bringing home a brace of brookies for the pan, I have no qualms about suggesting, when prevailing conditions seem to indicate its necessity, that you use a worm—or some other live bait.

The choice of live bait is endless. Almost anything that crawls, wiggles, swims or flies can be used to seduce brookies on occasion. A list of live baits that I have resorted to when fishing for brookies would include—besides worms—minnows, frogs, crawfish, grasshoppers, crickets, mayflies, newts, salamanders, maggots and assorted grubs.

Worms

. . . . . .

Using worms—dew worms, hybrid red worms or ordinary earthworms—is certainly the easiest way to fish in tiny quarters. Of course, a spinner can be lowered through the grasses and allowed to work its charm, but attempts to fish with a fly would only meet with profound frustration, although a small Muddler Minnow fly (simulating a grasshopper) or number 12 McGinty wet fly (looks like a bee) with a split shot to hold it down can occasionally induce a strike. But that is not fly-fishing per se. Negotiating swamps, especially cedar swamps, with their junglelike vines and atmosphere, while holding a fly rod in your hand is discouragement enough for even the most eager of wand wavers.

In most mini-flows, fishing with worms as bait can be every bit as much an art as presenting a dry fly to a rising trout on larger waters. In my youth I learned from my uncle that we were most successful when a medium-size, lively worm was simply fastened to the smallest hook in our tackle.

Q: *I think many well-kitted nimrods would be surprised to learn that in advocating worm usage, the Old Guy is actually following in the tradition of the godfather of fly-fishermen, Izaak Walton. In his classic,* The Compleat Angler, *Walton suggests that one use a* "worm, *which you may find under a Cow-tird."*

The worm should be threaded only once, through what is often described as the collar but is actually the egg sac, a darker and slightly thicker section near the worm's fatter end. The hook should be inserted in such a way that its eye is toward the shorter section of the worm. That will allow the worm to swim more naturally in the current while adding to its longevity. Hooking in the opposite direction tends to tear the worm apart more quickly. Use only enough weight—normally one or two small split shot—to allow the bait to drift naturally with the current.

The shot should be fastened at least 15 inches up the line. Inexplicably, on occasion and in certain streams, one can do better using only a tiny segment of worm, with the hook completely imbedded. Using the bait in this manner rarely requires more than a half-inch, preferably the tip.

One advantage for the segment angler is that the supply of bait should last longer than that of the whole-worm angler, which brings to mind the luck of trout fishermen in Australia. According to the *Guinness Book of Records,* that country is blessed with the world's longest earthworms, some, amazingly, exceeding 16 feet in length. One need only buy a single worm for a day of trout fishing in Australia and, of course, include a pair of scissors in one's gear.

> Q: *I feel I really must comment on this somewhat off-putting flight of Gordon's imagination. It is not uncharacteristic of the Old Guy. He has certain fancies, quips and jokes that he has at ready disposal. One of the most pleasant is, when he is asked how a day of fishing has been, to respond, "The fishing was excellent. The catching, however, left something to be desired." Another, less pleasant, occurs when a neophyte is driven to one of the fishing grounds on the Ganaraska. The trip involves driving through a little town called Osaka. Miles away, Gordon will start talking about a woman who lives there, one "Toomi," who will grant sexual favours for five dollars. He baits and goads the neophyte, asking if he wants to partake, etc. Usually the question is put just as we enter the village. "Are you being serious?" "Sure," Gordon will reply, "haven't you ever heard of Osaka Toomi?"*

Fishing for brookies in larger rivers, ponds and lakes often calls for a different set of guidelines altogether. With an appropriate lake bottom, hard and without too much bottom weed, a larger worm also hooked singularly through the egg sac can be allowed to wiggle around on the bottom without weights to detract from its natural appearance. In some situations this method of fishing with worms can be devastating—to the trout.

In waters containing considerably more bottom cover or weeds, a light balsa, cork or plastic float can be used to suspend the wiggler off the bottom. Usually the best results are obtained when the worm is allowed to send out its signals to the trout from a position just on the edge of the cover, rather than above or below it.

One of the best live-bait anglers I know, Rick Matusiak, consistently outfishes his mates by using worms in yet another manner. When fishing for brookies with spinning tackle in larger trout waters, if the usual hardware, spinners and wobblers prove to be a waste of time, Rick will often resort to casting a worm instead. Obviously, the cast must be more of a gentle lob, or the hook will go in one direction while the worm flies off in the opposite.

Rick will then fish the worm suspended over the weeds or cover, but rather than depending on the worm's innate seductiveness, he imparts a mild jigging motion to the bait with the tip of his rod. This also can be a fine way to stimulate otherwise uninterested and logy brookies into spectacular action.

Q: *Rick Matusiak is, indeed, one of the finest anglers I know. He was part of our quartet that went off to northern Quebec in search of the world's biggest brook trout. There was me, Gordon, Paul Kennedy and Matusiak. Rick is a quiet man, and a talented filmmaker, so he spent much of his nonfishing time working with his equipment and filming us. Kennedy, he and I also applied effort and energy to setting up a radio, in case disaster should befall us in the wild. We ran aerials way up into very tall trees (I say "we," but I mean the other guys) and then retrieved them and went up other trees. Finally, after days, we managed to get the thing working. We found a strong frequency and listened to a voice for many moments.*

"Works good," I noted.

"Works especially good," noted Rick, "if you speak French."

But fishing with a worm is one thing; hooking the fish—especially in tiny creeks and brooks with just a small piece of worm on your hook, a deadly method in small waters laden with thick beds of watercress—is another. The cress provides cool shelter for small brookies and usually hosts large numbers of aquatic larvae and insects that in most small waters provide the major portion of their table fare.

Drifting a healthy tidbit of worm into the cress beds offers any resident brookies another gourmet opportunity. Hooking an investigating trout in this situation calls for an almost instantaneous reaction, a sharp strike with the rod tip as soon as the bite is detected.

Any pause usually means that the fish will spit out the morsel the moment it feels the hook. Whereas quick reaction is necessary when fishing with pieces of worm, a whole worm necessitates patience.

Because the trout normally swim a few feet before inhaling the whole thing, they must be given the opportunity to move away with the worm, at which time the angler should execute the strike. With a little experience, this pattern is easily detected; however, if the angler strikes too quickly when fishing with a whole worm, more often than not it will simply be torn in two, providing the quarry with a free meal as it swims away with its half.

Other Live Bait
. . . .

Minnows form a substantial portion of the required sustenance for most fish and certainly most trout, especially the larger specimens. I believe, however, that using minnows as bait in small brooks and streams is completely unnecessary. Nevertheless, in rivers, ponds and lakes, where they are more likely to be a staple in a brook trout's diet, if fished properly, minnows can be highly productive.

Minnows can be fished in much the same manner as worms. When attaching them to the hook, take care not to touch the minnow's backbone with the hook point; that will kill the bait rather quickly and reduce your chances of a strike enormously. Whether you are fishing in a stream, river, pond or lake, the minnow should be as lively as possible if it is to interest your prey. Occasional exceptions to this rule are the exact opposite: either a dead minnow allowed to rest right on bottom (used where there are few natural minnows) or the crippled minnow ploy (the injured minnow tossed into a school of live minnows). The two generally preferred hooking methods are either through the minnow's lips from the bottom up (taking care not to hit the hard part of the bait's head) or, if you are still-fishing, through the back (above the backbone) right behind the dorsal fin.

If you have chosen the lip-hook method, a striking trout must be given ample time to move away and turn the bait—or sometimes to simply spit it out and grab it a second time—

before you attempt to set the hook. This is especially true if you are using very large minnows in bigger waters such as rivers and lakes. Under those circumstances the fish taking the bait must be given a count of fifteen or twenty steamboats (one steamboat, two steamboats, etc.) before you lift the rod sharply to set the hook.

Once again, striking too early with a lip-hooked minnow provides an easy repast for your trout. Fishing with a back-hooked minnow does require a faster strike, however, as the hook will usually enter the trout's mouth more quickly than will a lip-hooked bait.

Crickets and grasshoppers are more suitable fare in most of the smaller trout streams, which often wend their way through farms or meadows, where these insects are found in great numbers. They, too, should be fished with the smallest hook available and rigged to allow for the greatest movement without killing the insect. Crickets and grasshoppers naturally float, so when used as a lure they should be fished accordingly.

Crawfish are bottom dwellers and thus should be fished on or near the bottom, taking care that the critter does not swim completely beneath a rock and become snagged. It should be rigged with a slightly larger (number 8 to 10) hook inserted near the end of the tail and from the bottom, so that the point emerges on top facing the rear. Use only enough weight to allow you to control the bait's natural movements in the current.

I dislike using frogs as bait, since I find watching their almost humanlike attempts to pull themselves off the hooks rather unpleasant. But they are one of the more popular live baits and must be included here. Frogs are usually hooked through the lip, from the bottom up, or in one of the rear feet. The frog, fished in moderate depths, must be allowed to swim freely.

When using crawfish and frogs as live bait, you must allow enough time for the trout taking the bait to swim away with it a few feet before setting the hook. The shape, feel and size of these live baits seem to impart little concern to a trout attacking them, even when they are fastened to a hook. Thus, you have ample time to allow the trout to take the entire bait and hook into its mouth, increasing your chances of success in hooking the fish.

Newts and salamanders, those little lizardlike creatures, although more suitable as bait for brown trout, will also take brookies, especially larger fish in medium-size streams. They, too, should be rigged and fished in much the same manner as crawfish.

I had a memorable experience when fishing with a newt. It occurred on a second honeymoon trip with my wife to New York City. After four or five days of doing the Big Apple, I was able to convince her that we should escape the mad tempo, dirt and confusion of that great city and make the two-hour drive north into the Catskill Mountains. I had just finished reading an article in *Field and Stream* about trout fishing in the Beaverkill River and one of its famous tributaries, the Willowemoc. The gist of the article was that the author had camped beside one of the last remaining covered bridges in America, which just happened to cross the Willowemoc, and fly-fished the surrounding waters, taking a couple of decent browns during the evening stonefly hatch.

I showed my wife the story and photos of the picturesque covered bridge and said that it might be fun to have a look at the place. She bought my suggestion. I am sure she understood, though, that I had an ulterior motive, as I had been fiddling with my fishing tackle on and off for several days.

The next evening found us checking the many motel and

cabin facilities around the village of Roscoe, deep in the heart of the Catskills, in an attempt to locate accommodation for the night. There was none. It appeared that every fisherman in New York had read the same story, because all the hotels had NO ROOMS AVAILABLE signs prominently displayed. But I am a stubborn bugger and not easily deterred once my mind is made up to do something.

Fortunately, before leaving Toronto, I had tossed a couple of sleeping bags into the back of the car for just such an occasion. In addition, the car was equipped with folding front seats, which when unlatched and turned down made an ideal bed for the bags. I pointed the car up the winding road leading to the Willowemoc and in short order was parked by the large pool on the upstream side of the covered bridge.

The evening was pitch black—cloudy and moonless. The outline of the bridge was barely discernible, and before I was even able to set up the beds and unroll the sleeping bags, I heard a large *plop* coming from 20 feet away in the pool. It was so loud that I mistakenly assumed it must have been made by a beaver smacking its tail on the surface after becoming annoyed by our car's headlights.

Plop! There it was again, just as we had undressed and were about to climb into the sleeping bags. *Plop!* Very unnerving—it was even louder.

"I wonder if that could be a big trout, not a beaver," I said to myself. "Damn, I've got to find out."

When I told my wife where I was going, she said I must be nuts and please don't wake her up when I come back to the car. I scrambled around in the dark with only a tiny flashlight to help me locate and set up my spinning rod. Setting up a fly rod in those conditions seemed like an even more foolish thing to do.

Plop!

Damn! I cursed again as I removed the point of the barb from my thumb, into which I had inadvertently yanked the spinner's hook after the last splash. By then I was convinced that it had indeed been made by a big trout and not a beaver.

As my eyesight gradually adjusted to the blackness of the night, I was able to discern the receding rings on the surface of the pool that distinctly indicated where whatever it was had made that last jump. I sucked my thumb for a moment or two and fired the spinner into the middle of the rapidly diminishing circles, ignoring, at least for a couple of casts, my wife's urgent pleas to return to the car and sleeping bags, while continuing what was rapidly developing into a fruitless exercise.

Assuring her that I would be along in a moment (har-de-har-har!), I continued to work the pool with the spinner. But when the water erupted again near the opposite side and I was able to land the lure precisely on target a split second later without any reaction from whatever it was, I began to think that maybe it was just a playful beaver after all. I capitulated, hanging my head in defeat as I carefully picked my way back to the car with the help of the little flashlight beam aimed at the ground.

The beam momentarily caught something glistening and scurrying out of the intruding light.

Probably a dew worm, I thought. Then I thought, maybe I should see if I can find one, hook it on the spinner and toss it out and see what happens.

A brief search failed to produce any worms in the immediate area, but when I flipped a rock over, a prettily coloured newt cowered in the flashlight beam. I grabbed it instinctively, hooked it through the tail and lobbed the creature to what I hoped would be an interesting fate. The lure with its cargo splashed down in the middle of the pool, creating an even bigger splash than its quarry—but I did not have long to wait this time. The whole apparition was promptly engulfed and then all hell broke loose.

I yelled for my wife to get out of the sack and come and see the fun, but she refused to budge, repeating her pleas for me to hurry up and get back to the car. The whatever it was turned out to be a trout, all right, and a big one. Unfortunately, it was not a brookie but a 22-inch-long brown trout.

I dispatched it, wrapped it in the *New York Times,* placed it in the cooler with the cans of pop and plastic jug of ice and went to bed contented and looking forward to more of the same in the morning. The remainder of this little tale appears in Chapter Two of Part 2.

> Q: *Yes, that's a good story, and it reminds me of something characteristic of the Old Guy's fishing style. You recall how he jammed one of the treble hooks into his thumb? He blamed the darkness in this case, but the truth of the matter is he does that sort of stuff all the time. He's always finding some way of hurting himself, and to spend time with Gordon is to hear a series of pained invective. He actually swears like they do in the funny pages, "$@#!"—that sort of thing.*

Mayflies were included in the list of live baits that could be used to catch trout. Having only used them once myself, I am nevertheless aware that there is a method of using them as bait while fishing for brown trout in lakes in Ireland, referred to as "dapping." Very long and light rods equipped with gossamer lines and the tiniest of dry fly hooks are used to float the fragile mayflies in the breeze downwind from drifting boats, allowing them with a little slack to alight momentarily (dap) on the surface.

This is repeated continuously, simulating the real-life mating and egg-laying dances of other mayflies without hooks up their rear. I have never taken the time and trouble to rig equipment to give this technique a trial for brookies and browns in our own waters, but I did use mayflies successfully in a considerably different manner once.

We were fishing for pickerel, below the bridge and dam in the village of Hastings, Ontario, and the customary offerings of streamer flies or jigs seemed incapable of tweaking their fancy. We remained fishless until the live-bait bug bit me again. It seems that whenever a fisherman's conventional procedures fail to produce action, his thoughts turn to live bait. Mine are no exception. Although we regularly used worms, frogs or minnows to catch pickerel, we had none of them in our possession and the local bait store was sold out as well.

The weather had been unusually hot and humid for mid-May, resulting in the heaviest hatch of lovely, large olive-coloured mayflies I have ever seen. The main road, inundated with the fluttering insects during the mayfly invasion, continues directly across the bridge over the Trent River. The orgy of reproduction that we had been witnessing had a downside, however, as car after car crossing the bridge came perilously close to sliding through the railing and plunging into the river. It was as if the insects were getting retribution for being crushed. If local residents had not been standing at each end of the bridge cautioning approaching drivers to slow down, one or more autos would have gone for the deep six beneath the bridge in the rushing Trent River.

It occurred to me that perhaps the reason we were not catching anything was that the pickerel were gorging on both the larvae as they emerged from the river bottom and the live mayflies on the surface—when they were able to catch them. I tied on a number 2 long-shank hook, weighted it 2 feet up from the hook with a number 4 clincher sinker, then, scooping up a handful of the olive-coloured insects, fastened them one by one onto the hook until its entire length was covered with fluttering and wiggling mayflies.

It probably required a couple of dozen to do the job, but it seemed somehow to offer them a better fate than being eradicated by automobiles. In very short order my buddy and I had our limit of six fat pickerel, and most of the other folks fishing around us who had witnessed our success soon adapted to the buggy bait and also filled their stringers.

> Q: *Gordon's relationship with the pickerel is a bit standoffish. He's openly scornful of pike, but the Old Guy seems to be able to accept the concept of pickerel, probably because they taste so good. And he can cook them so well. On our last trip to northern Quebec, I was able to say those words that I thought would never pass my lips, coming as I do from these southern parts, where the fish have become very sparse indeed. I was able to say (wiping my lips), "All right, that's enough, no more pickerel for me."*

Grubs and maggots have also been used successfully in all seasons. (See Chapter Two of Part 2 for more on this topic.) Stories about their use are legion. My favourite is the myth that this obnoxious live bait must be kept warm in the mouth of the angler before it is fastened to the hook, ostensibly to keep it alive and wiggling well. Yuck! Yet I know for a fact that the practice has been followed religiously by members of a few cultures, such as Scandinavian ice fishermen.

I have never used maggots as bait but have had limited success in using them on a lake as chum to attract brook trout to a specific area, where they could then be fished for in a more conventional manner. This involved obtaining a small dead animal, either a groundhog or porcupine, usually off a highway shoulder, then suspending it over the water near shore on a cord attached to an overhanging branch.

> Q: *All right, all right, I know I should do something here in my capacity as commentator/editor. Um, it seems like the Old Guy has been stringing up road kill over the ice and letting maggots drop down into the hole. Well, Gordon does have a more personal relationship with road kill than many, if not all other, people. He'll be driving along, and although his eyes seemed fastened on the world lying ahead, from time to time his head will jerk around and he'll say, "There's a dead fox in that ditch over there." And then he'll back up (even if we're on a superhighway) and toss the fox into his trunk and go about his business. I suppose he uses the fur for fly-tying, and now we know about the over-the-ice suspension. Beyond that, I don't ask a lot of questions about this behaviour.*

I believe any kind of grub, properly fished, will help put trout, especially brookies, in your creel. I have even used grubs that we scrounged out of the pretty ripe cow dung that is easily located beside many trout streams. It sounds disgusting, but it works. Another unusual grub that can often be found quite close to trout streams can be dug out with a pocketknife from the golf-ball-size swellings that occur on the stalks of milkweed plants in late spring and early summer.

Maggots and grubs must be fished with the lightest and smallest hooks available. Fine-wire dry fly hooks are perfect for this exercise.

Because they enter a trout's mouth much more quickly than a larger bait does, grubs, maggots, grasshoppers or any other type of tiny live bait usually require a quick reactionary strike from the angler. The fisherman who takes the time to learn to fish with live bait properly, attempting to present his offerings in as natural a manner as possible, will undoubtedly experience gratification in the knowledge that he, too, must be considered as much an angler as the best of fly-fishermen. Fishing correctly with live bait can be considered every bit as much of an art form as skillful fly-fishing.

Although I have attempted to show that using live bait to catch fish, if properly done, is not the simple utilitarian exercise that it is popularly believed to be, I must admit that I prefer to fish for brookies with artificial flies or lures whenever conditions permit.

Q: *We knew this, Gordon old tit. That's what he calls me, sometimes—old tit—so I thought I'd get back at him forever by calling him that in print. Anyway, let's get out those lures and learn how to fish from the Old Guy.*

CHAPTER THREE

Catching Brookies on Artificial Lures

. . . .

*A*lmost from the time humans discovered that fish were good to eat, artificial lures have been used as enticements. No doubt the fisherman who first learned that his accuracy with a spear was not enough to guarantee a fish for dinner every night also discovered that fish were attracted to shiny pieces of shell and other bits of flotsam and jetsam wobbling in the water as they sank to the bottom. These, or small pieces of other fish, were probably simply used as an attractor, or chum, to bring his quarry closer for an even better shot at the potential feast with his spear. Although archaeologists have discovered barbed fish hooks made from two pieces of sharpened wood or bamboo fastened together with pieces of thong made from animal hide, the earliest recorded artificial lures with a crudely fashioned hook attached showed up much later.

Fashioned from clamshells, artificial lures with a beautiful mother-of-pearl finish can still be purchased in many tackle shops. They use the natural curve of the shell to provide the necessary resistance when they are pulled through the water. It is this resistance to pressure that causes spinners to spin and wobblers to wobble. Special equipment is necessary to drill holes in shell, and the better-made lures have a brass grommet inserted in the holes to reinforce them.

Mother-of-pearl shell is used to make small blades for spinners, bigger, elongated blades for spinning lures and even larger ones for the 3- to 6-inch wobblers used by fishermen trolling for large brookies and lake trout. One of the most productive spinning lures I ever owned was a 2-inch-long wobbler fashioned from mother-of-pearl on the outside with an inner skin of hammered and polished brass that had been carefully riveted to its inside, concave surface.

This wobbler, or spoon, as some anglers prefer to call it, was called an M.O.P. spoon and was produced in Switzerland, where some of the finest spinning lures are still made. It could easily have been mistaken for a lovely piece of jewellery—if it had not been equipped with a fine French treble hook. Probably several dozen or more brookies fell for the charms of this lure before I hung it up irretrievably on the bottom of one of my favourite brook trout fisheries, Mosque Lake, in eastern Ontario.

If after reading this treatise on lures manufactured from mother-of-pearl you find yourself searching the tackle shops for one to try out on your own special lake or river, look it over carefully, since, like fingerprints, no two are alike. You should try to find one that is perfectly symmetrical so that it will wobble, not spin. Locating the perfect shape may not be the easiest thing to do, but should you be lucky enough to find one, you may be amply rewarded. It also seems that the more iridescent the finish, the more attractive it is to trout.

If the blade—whether it be a spinner or a spoon—is not uniformly shaped, it will be out of balance and not work correctly when retrieved. That is, the spinners will not spin at all on a slow retrieve and the wobblers will spin instead of wobbling from side to side at most speeds of retrieve. An improperly balanced lure means fewer fish on the stringer.

> Q: *I did a magazine article on this very subject, i.e., lures and why they work. I talked to scientists as well as anglers and learned some very interesting things. The discussion that was most eye-opening to me concerned a fish's lateral line, which I knew about from reading angling books and magazines but never really understood. Fish actually have an extra sense in that line running the length of their bodies. "We can never really understand what it's like, of course," said one scientifical type, "but try to imagine that you're standing in a room and someone comes in, and without seeing or hearing him, you know he's there." So motion, vibration, etc., become very important when fishing with lures. Therefore, always make sure they're spinning or wobbling properly.*

History suggests that wobblers were the first artificial fishing lures, but carved wooden plugs were not far behind. Like many modern plugs, they were shaped and in some cases even coloured to resemble minnows and other assorted bait fish such as suckers and herring. The first of these, too, were probably just used as decoys to bring fish close enough to be easily speared. They naturally evolved into what are now called plugs with hooks attached.

Plugs are seldom used in fishing for brookies, however, though there are exceptions to this rule. Case in point: On a trip with our fishing and casting club to A/B Lake in Haliburton to fish for brookies a couple of years ago, the trout were proving to be most uncooperative; a dozen of us supposedly ace anglers (well, experienced anyhow) were basically skunked when a tiny balsa plug broke the impasse. Good friend and fishing buddy Roger Cannon, president of Normark Canada, one of the premier fishing tackle importers in Canada, had stowed his fly-fishing tackle, set up a spinning rod and fastened a little plug (Rapala) he had just received as a sample from Finland to his monofilament. An hour or so later he trolled by our boat as we were still flailing away with fly lines at the shoreline and held up a brace of gorgeous 20-inch brookies for us to admire. Nevertheless, I firmly believe that wobblers, spinners and flies will outfish plugs 95 per cent of the time when one is angling for brook trout.

Most often I adhere to this general guideline: spinners in moving waters such as brooks, streams, rivers; wobblers in ponds and lakes.

Spinners
. . . .

The best spinners in the world, Mepps and Vibrax, are made in France and Finland. In all conditions a silver finish—actually rhodium in most cases—will outfish all others, while those adorned with paint or a decal in a colour that reacts to ultraviolet, usually referred to as fire-orange, fire-red, and so on, will occasionally produce well in low light or murky waters.

Leave spinners dressed with bucktail or feathered treble hooks on the shelves in the tackle shops. These adornments do not add in any way to the lure's desirability to trout and even detract from its allure.

Many hours of snorkelling with a 2-foot-long ice-fishing rod in one hand have given my fishing buddies and me the opportunity to study and compare the various spinners from a trout's underwater perspective. Some fascinating determinations have been made as a result.

From a brookie's position in the water, a spinner blade does not appear to be revolving, as it only reflects light above the body of the lure in one specific position during its revolutions around the wire shank. The precise position depends on the relative location of the sun or the brightest area in the sky if it is cloudy. With the weighted body and hook hanging lower in the water than the portion of the blade reflecting light, a correctly worked spinner resembles a fluttering butterfly in the water.

Brookies—and all other types of trout—will strike a properly fished spinner for a variety of reasons: its overall silhouette and appearance, the light flashing off the silver blade and, perhaps most importantly, the vibrations emitted by both the resistance factor of the blade as it spins and with the higher-frequency vibrations caused by the edge of the blade as it cuts through the water in its revolutions around the lure shank. A spinner blade with a nickel or chrome finish reflects far less light than does one plated with silver or rhodium. In some light conditions these inferior finishes appear black when viewed underwater. The silver finish also comes much closer to matching the natural colouration of shiners and many other bait fish.

On occasion I have been known to bite the bullet, grab a handful of my spinners and lures, cart them to a jewellery store and have them all plated with a silver finish. This is an expensive proposition but certainly worth it when your box of lures lose their lustre. The only drawback to the silver finishes is that in time they will tarnish; merely rubbing them for a moment or two on your sleeve restores their lustre, however.

Q: *I never knew that, about Gordon taking his lures to a jewellery store. I knew that he is ever reluctant to lend them to me, and this might explain why. Because I lose lures, you know. I lose a lotta lotta lures. And much of my time on the river—this is something left out of the Introduction—is spent in lure retrieval. Sometimes it's possible to wade out in the river, reach down amongst the tree roots (wetting your arm from finger to shoulder) and pull the lure free. You ruin the hole, of course, so often what happens at a spot is the Old Guy and I will creep up on it. He'll point to an undercut on the far bank. I will toss my lure into a nearby tree. I then pull my rod away to clear the line as well as possible, and Gordon will fire to the undercut. It's almost a ritual.*

Spinners made with narrow or elongated willow-leaf-type blades produce less resistance, as do those equipped with smaller blades, and therefore sink quickly. Those constructed with larger, wider or more oval shaped blades offer considerably more lure control and a wider range of retrieval speeds.

Spinning lures such as the phenomenally successful French Vibrax spinner and the older Mepps spinners are perfectly balanced and can be worked correctly at any reasonable speed. The Vibrax even has a built-in counterrevolutionary system; the shank and body revolve in one direction, while the spinner rotates in the opposite fashion.

As with any lure, however, if it is drawn through the water too rapidly, the resistance of the blade and clevis on the shaft becomes so great that the entire lure revolves, imparting an unfortunate twist to the line. Therefore, other than at extremely slow speeds, trolling with spinners should be avoided. Spinners are primarily designed to be used as casting lures.

A spinner blade with sharp, right-angled edges produces a great deal more vibration in the water than does one that has been tumbled to smooth the edges and make it look more attractive to the fishermen purchasing it. Only spinners with so-called French hooks—those needle-pointed, bronze-finished trebles—should be used. Shiny nickel-plated hooks detract from the lure's effectiveness. After all, why attract attention to the hooks?

A number of years ago I was asked to testify before the Supreme Court of Canada in a lengthy action that had been brought about by the importer of one of the aforementioned French spinners against a gentleman who was buying them in quantity and bringing them into the country on his own. He owned a small tackle shop and sold the lures much more cheaply than if he had had to get his stock from the importer.

I spent three days in Ottawa testifying about every detail of the spinner's construction and why it is superior to its myriad imitators. As a so-called expert witness, when cross-examined, I simply justified my position by stating that I was an ardent trout fisherman who held a couple of records and did a little writing on angling topics, as well as being an angler with a very analytical mind who had studied and tested every spinner that could be purchased in Canada at that time.

Although I enjoyed every moment of the trial (our side won and the shop owner continued to circumvent the importer), I noticed that almost all the bewigged judges were nodding off at regular intervals during my "complicated" testimony. There were a couple of gentlemen on the bench though who did express a considerable amount of interest in the details I was elaborating on, such as the finish, shape and edges of various spinners on the market.

There were samples of most of them for the judges to peruse while I elaborated on their fine and not-so-fine points. I suppose the judges who remained awake and whose interest I managed to pique were fishermen when they were not on duty on the bench. I mention my experience in that court case simply to emphasize that there are great differences between good spinners and those of poor quality and performance.

> Q: *No doubt about it, Gordon knows his spinners. I'll often pull something out of one of my ugly jacket's many pockets (see Introduction), some spinner bait I've elected to try, and the Old Guy will grab it out of my hand, hold it up and peer at it for many long moments. He'll inspect it from all angles. He'll raise a finger and spin the blade. The Old Guy might make a few adjustments, and he'll certainly tear away any flash, feather or plastic tubing that might be "decorating" the shaft. Then he'll grunt and hand it back, and I'll tie it on and shoot it up into a tree. It's a ritual.*

Like most fishing lures, spinners should not simply be tossed out and reeled in. The angler who takes a moment to study the water he is about to fish, who seeks out the cover—or, more likely, the holding locations (places where the trout dwell for the most part)—before making a precise cast as close to the trout as possible and who imparts lifelike variety to his lure's action will always catch more trout than will the average fisherman.

One of the biggest factors that differentiates the successful angler from the fellow who perennially returns empty-handed is that the chap with the full creel more than likely has learned not to depend on the inherent action of the lure alone. He knows that the lure should not simply be reeled in after a cast but retrieved with the rod tip in a variety of twitches, sweeps and so on, inducing the lure to change speeds and depths accordingly. Feeling the current's pressure on the lure allows him to speed up or slow down the retrieve and adjust the action to suit the conditions. An angler who attempts to think like the trout he is pursuing will always have better luck than the non-imaginative fisherman.

When you are fishing in small creeks and streams for brookies, accurate casting skills are paramount if you are to entice these fish into leaving their cover to investigate and strike the fluttering intruder in their field of view. It is equally important if your cast is short of the mark to get it back out of the water immediately, even if you have to yank it out with a jerk that places your ears in peril. Should a brookie come out for a look-see at the lure that drops too far from its lair, by the time the fish catches up to it the spinner will be in water that is too shallow or even at your feet. The trout pursuing the lure will head back to its cover almost instantly and more than likely will refuse to show again when upset in this manner.

Many fishermen swear that a spinner with a worm dangling off the hook will produce more action than will the lure itself. I stick by my belief that a worm is best fished on its own—as is a spinner—providing the suggestions (rules) for their respective usage are adhered to. Nevertheless, when one is fishing for certain species other than trout, such as pickerel and bass, a spinner-and-worm combination may prove successful.

Although I have had great luck fishing with wobblers for brookies in larger bodies of water, in brooks and streams they have never proven to be as productive as the French spinners.

Q: *You note those parentheses up there: "suggestions (rules)." This is kind of indicative of the Old Guy's mentality. He runs the Scarborough Fly and Bait Casting Association as a benevolent dictator, and several members have balked, finally, at having been made to adhere to suggestions (rules). Many, for example, are reluctant to chop the bails off their*

casting reels, their attitude being this is a fine piece of equip-
ment that cost me a pretty penny, that thing there must do
something useful or they wouldn't have put it on, so why
should I chop it off? Gordon won't throw anyone out of the
club for a failure to chop off the bail, but as the rebel stands in
the gym casting at the firebells (all this shall be explained in
time) the Old Guy will deal him a withering glance and not
point out the flaws in his technique.

Wobblers

. . . .

Nevertheless, using a small, ½- to 1-inch-long wobbler, such as another Swiss-made lure, the E.G.B., or Halfwave, can produce action in some slower and deeper streams. Such lures should be stamped out of metal at least .065 inch in thickness if one is going to be able to work them properly. If the wobblers are too light, they tend to spin rather than work from side to side, thereby building an unwanted twist to the monofilament line.

For the same reason, the holes punched in the lures where the line or split rings are attached must be perfectly centred to retain the lure's balance in the water. The closer the line is fastened to a wobbler, the greater the resistance of the water when it is being retrieved, resulting in superior lure action. Therefore, if you must use a snap swivel or split ring, it should be as small as possible.

For maximum lure action, providing the edges of the hole are not sharp, the line should be tied directly to the wobbler with a double-improved clinch knot. This technique provides the angler with another advantage. Because a few inches of line are broken off each time a lure is changed, fresh, unworn line is moved up to the terminal end.

Many fishermen using a snap swivel to fasten their lures become rather careless in this department. Most of the wear and tear on a fisherman's line is in the last few inches, resulting from friction caused by the tip guide of the rod, along with the lure's—and line's—scuffing against rocks on the bottom.

Using snap swivels in an attempt to avoid line twist is a useless exercise anyhow, because when placed under tension, even the finest of this hardware does not perform that function efficiently. The truth of this statement is easily illustrated by an interesting little exercise. Fasten one end of a snap swivel to something or another and the other end to a taut elastic with a 3-inch pencil in it at the other end (see fig. 1, below). Wind up the elastic using the pencil, and you will immediately see that the swivel does not swivel as it is supposed to: the elastic twists and tightens.

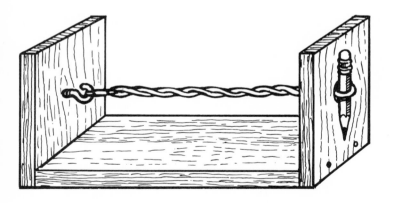

fig. 1: TESTING A SNAP SWIVEL

Q: *This is the kind of experiment that Gordon comes up with down in his basement. That basement is truly one of the wonders of the world. As I pointed out in my little book* Fishing With My Old Guy, *if you have ever lost a piece of angling equipment, I know where it is. Down there, in one of countless old tackle boxes or crates or plastic containers. Buried beneath all this are a couple of work benches with strange machines affixed to them, line reelers and tying vices. Hidden in the shadows is a huge deep freezer where Gordon keeps his specimens.*

So it is no problem at all for Gordon to find a snap swivel, fasten it to something or another (that's all he has down there, somethings or anothers) and attach the other end to an elastic band (Gordon collects elastic bands com-pulsively) with a 3-inch pencil at the other end. I'm not sure I follow, really, but the swivel doesn't swivel as it's supposed to, and I guess we'll all just take his word on that, huh?

For some reason or another, wobblers used in these situa-tions will put more brookies in the frying pan if they are con-structed with darker finishes. Bronze spoons (wobblers) or those in dark colour combinations seem to be more effective than the silver finishes that work best with spinners, probably because those wobblers are more likely to resemble dark chub and sucker minnows or crawfish. The same rules suggested here for fishing spinners in trout streams (accuracy, working the lure, etc.) are also applicable to wobblers.

In brook trout lakes, such as those in Ontario's Algonquin Park and Haliburton areas, and in large rivers like the famous Nipigon, where the overall world record brook trout was caught in 1914, or Quebec's mighty Broadback, larger silver-finished elongated lures can work miracles. The same specifics of construction apply as for the smaller wobblers—heavy-gauge metal blades, perfectly proportioned and balanced, with French treble hooks.

Whereas there is a dearth of good spinners to be found in the shops, there are many fine wobblers that meet the criteria suggested in these paragraphs. Once again, avoid the nickel and chrome finishes and purchase only wobblers with silver or contrasting colour combinations if you want superior results.

The best of these slim, elongated wobblers are designed in the familiar Crocodile lure shape of the original, the Swedish Delphin Crocodile. A lure that I designed based on the same lines is easily the best of its many imitators. The Gord Deval Crocodile contains about a dozen features making it a superior lure. Unfortunately, only a limited number were made. If you are lucky enough to locate one, you will find an insert boxed with the lure explaining the features that make this an exceptional wobbler.

Q: *I think I still have a Gord Deval Crocodile, somewhere. (I shouldn't make too much fun of Gordon's basement; you ought to see my storage room.) I used to have several of them, but over the years I distributed them amongst various submerged rocks and overhanging branches.*

Once I was fishing with some friends, still-fishing, bait-fishing for pickerel (that most Canadian of activities, even though the Old Guy doesn't care for it), and we began to be bothered by a marauding pike. He would tear along the bottom of the lake gleefully (so I imagined, anyway) tearing off our minnows, spitting out the hooks, so I looked in my tackle box to see what I could catch the guy on, and my eyes lit upon the Gord Deval Crocodile. It was brand new, I remember, still in its box, presented to me by the inventor only a few days before. Let's see how good this thing works,

I thought, and I tied it on and tossed it out and bang-zoom I had the pike. (Bang-zoom, by the way, is truly the way a pike encounter takes place.)

A few days later, at the weekly club meeting, I told the Old Guy that his lure worked great.

"Excellent! What did you catch?"

I instantly saw the folly of my lack of forethought. I opened my mouth to speak, but could find no words.

I have never seen him so disappointed. Gordon's face seemed to melt, his eyes fairly welled with tears. "Aw," he moaned, "you didn't catch a pike, didya?"

I didn't answer; he turned away. We spoke no more of it.

There have probably been more fish, including brook trout, lake trout and rainbows, caught over the years on red and white Daredevil spoons than all the other wobblers put together. The original of these, the Lou Eppinger Daredevil, is probably still the best of these old standbys. All fishermen are familiar with the spoon, with its white swoosh on a red background. Although Daredevil spoons will certainly catch fish, especially large fish on the bigger models, I think they are popular for the same reason that Coca-Cola is—they are everywhere—available in a huge array of sizes, colours and prices and made by fishing tackle companies in almost every country in the world. Daredevils can be found in almost every fisherman's tackle box, but not mine.

A Final Bit of Advice

. . . .

All the odds are in the fish's favour to begin with; therefore, if an angler is to have a reasonable chance of success, those odds must be reduced as much as possible. Accordingly, when

fishing for brook trout, my fishing buddies and I seldom experiment, preferring to stick with the lures that we know will produce better results—most of the time.

My equipment does not include a tackle box anymore. It
hasn't for many years, ever since I learned that you only need
the essential spinners and wobblers discussed here. The time
wasted by fishermen changing lures, over and over again, seeking a winner, would be much more profitably spent with their
lure—any lure—working in the water.

We simply carry our lures in a couple of pocket-sized plastic
boxes, or if we are stream-fishing for brookies with spinning
tackle, all that is necessary is one or two of those clear plastic
35mm film containers. Nevertheless, some folks take great
pleasure in collecting everything that is made in the name of
fishing tackle.

Jack Wilkings, a fishing buddy of mine since the fifties, who,
sadly, passed away a few years ago, was the exception that
proved the rule. He owned what probably was the biggest
tackle box in the world, a multi-trayed cantilevered monstros-
ity that contained several tiers of removable trays that in
themselves held more than any tackle box I ever possessed or
even saw until Jack's came along.

As a matter of fact, it didn't just come along. My old buddy
owned a stainless steel fabrication company, and the box, which
to begin with was the largest obtainable from one of the
biggest companies making them, was refitted in his plant to
hold Jack's enormous collection of lures. Not only was he ob-
sessed with owning every lure that was ever made, but one was
not enough for him—he had to have at least two of each and
would purchase the better lures by the dozen.

After Jack passed away, I had the unpleasant task of assisting his wife, Doris, with the task of evaluating his massive col-

lection of tackle. The box and its contents were conservatively appraised at $2,200. Jack owned more Gord Deval Crocodiles than I had ever had in my possession, and his stock of E.G.B.s and other exotic spinning lures exceeded by far what could be found in any sporting goods store in Toronto.

Nevertheless, the gentlemen forming my current corps of fishing buddies all seem to agree that as far as possessing fishing lures goes, less is better. Even on a two-week trip into northern Quebec to fish the magnificent Broadback River for giant brook trout, none of us carries more than a couple of dozen spinners, in addition to an assortment of trout flies and a few Crocodiles and small Swiss wobblers.

The exception, once again, was my good friend Roger Cannon, who in his position with Normark Canada obviously has the responsibility to take with him and make at least a few token casts with each of the lures his company imports from France and Finland. Nevertheless, on that particular Quebec trip, Roger used his silver Vibrax spinners more than anything else, catching a number of "mounties" (trout over 20 inches) on that excellently constructed lure.

Fishing for Brookies with Fur & Feather

. . . .

There has probably been more written about fly-fishing for trout than about any other subject dealing with the sport of angling. If you have a fat wallet and are willing to do a little research, you can still buy books on this topic dating back to the sixteenth century in rare book stores. Old buddy Jack Wilkings owned a fine collection of ancient treatises on fly-fishing. One of his books, written by an English lady–fly-fisher, was published in 1586.

The language used in these early works is barely decipherable by an angler today, but it does not take a scholar to determine that much of what has been written in the past about fly-fishing for trout is still pertinent today. These works were, of course, written in Europe, mainly by English and Scottish angler-authors.

As far as I have been able to determine, the earliest books written on the subject in North America, mostly by authors in the northeastern fishing areas of the United States, were printed in the late nineteenth century. After brown trout were exported from Europe to North America, however, the field exploded, and all sorts of "experts" wrote millions of words on every phase that they could think of, or imagine, to do with fly-fishing.

Although the original German brown trout is generally credited with being the most responsive of all trout to an artificial fly, fly-fishing anglers discovered long ago that our own North American piscatorial pleasure-treasure, *Salvelinus fontinalus,* brook trout, can also be quite receptive to fur and feather.

Trout flies—specifically, flies for brookies—basically fall into one of four classes: nymphs, streamers, wet flies and the classic—dry flies. I find it an interesting phenomenon that when the subject of angling comes up in general conversation with a non-aficionado and you happen to mention that you are a trout fisherman, he or she will almost always respond with a statement such as the following: "Then you must be a fly-fisherman."

Even before you can respond, your questioner will usually continue: "You know, I've watched it on TV. Saw it in that movie, too, you know, something about a river. It looks like fun, but I guess it's pretty difficult, eh?"

I will restrain myself from yelling, and politely explain, "Yeah, as a matter of fact, I am a fly-fisherman, but I also fish for trout with a spinning rod, using spinners and wobblers, and sometimes, if I can't catch them that way, my buddies and I will even use live bait."

Normally I will add: "Hey, you're not alone. Although most people think that you have to be a fly-fisherman to catch trout, you don't, but fly-fishing does reward the angler with a number of perks not available to other anglers and is definitely my angling method of choice *when the conditions permit its use.*"

Long ago I gave up fly-fishing for brookies unless there was room to cast where I was planning to fish. There are several reasons for this. With dense overhanging foliage and branches, a comparatively weightless fly on the end of a fine leader is almost impossible to properly present to your quarry. Should you somehow manage to get the thing in the water and entice a brookie, chances are that you will miss the strike because of the extremely short overhang of line and leader in conjunction with the longer-than-average rods used for fly-fishing. When that happens, you have to extricate not just your fly from the branches but the flimsy leader as well—and sometimes even the tip of your fly rod. Fishing is supposed to be fun—that sort of exercise is simply frustration!

Nevertheless when there is room to make even short casts without having to climb trees every few minutes, we generally prefer to use fly tackle. There are a couple of other exceptions to that, though, as well.

If the waters are too muddied or roiled, as is often the case after heavy rains, I will also choose to throw tin, usually spinners, rather than fly-fish. And very early in the season before the bug hatches and the mosquitoes and black flies erupt, I will also go with the spinning outfit most of the time.

At the risk of offending the many folks who fancy themselves the elite of the angling world because they own a couple of fly rods and actually do fish with flies on occasion (I have seen fly-fishermen using worms on their fly tackle and, on other outings, attempting to fly-fish with a spinning lure tied to the end of their flimsy leaders) I must reiterate that the sport of fly-fishing is not the be-all or end-all of the angling world. It is a great way to fish when conditions permit, but fishing with spinning tackle and lures will almost always prove to be more productive, certainly in numbers if not in pure pleasure.

Q: *All right, let me try to explain something of the Old Guy's somewhat complex attitude toward this whole fly-fishing thing. Here we find him railing against the*

*snobbery that is, undoubtedly, rampant in the angling
world. Well-kitted nimrods do indeed look down their noses
at fishermen who pull trout out of creeks using artificials
and (worse) live bait. Even bass fishermen, outfitted with
winches filled with 20-pound test and jigs tipped with pork
rind—even those guys think badly of us. But I'd like to
make a couple of points.*

*1) Heavy-brush spin-casting is every bit as challenging,
I think, as fly-casting.*

*2) When Gordon says, "It is a great way to fish when
conditions permit," he actually means, "It is a great way to
fish when it's just barely physically possible." Thus you find
him standing beside a river, fly rod at the ready, turning
around with a pleasantly baffled look on his face, grinning
merrily when he spies a little hole in the canopy behind
him, a hole big enough to receive his line on the back cast,
small enough to permit no mistake. You also find Gordon
fly-fishing in huge rivers, the racing water licking at the top
of his chestwaders, his arms held up and working line furiously. One manner in which he fly-fishes, which he makes
look easy but I which find damnably hard, is whilst sitting
in a canoe. Gordon will effortlessly execute a double-haul
(more of this coming) throwing the fly far, far away, without even rocking the canoe.*

Fly-Casting
. . . .

You do not require the expertise of a competitive tournament
caster to enjoy fly-fishing, but being comfortable with your
equipment and technique enables you to obtain pleasure from
the sport whether the trout are hitting or not. A fly-fisherman
who has mastered the art of laying a dry fly down on the surface

exactly where he wishes, gently enough that it appears natural to a feeding brookie—and, when necessary, being able to cast 80, 90 or even more than 100 feet—can truly maximize that pleasure.

Anyone wishing to take up fly-fishing should seek advice and instruction from an expert fly-caster, preferably one from a casting club, such as my own, the Scarborough Fly and Bait Casting Association. Most casting clubs have a number of fly-fishermen who are tournament casters or ex-tournament casters, and most clubs are willing to spend time with new people, whether they become members or not.

Although this book is not intended to be a manual on tournament casting, I am including a description of double-haul casting, an invaluable tool in a fly-fisherman's arsenal of casting essentials and techniques. Mastering the double-haul enables one to make casts of remarkable distances with little effort and to make shorter accurate casts without having to wave the line and rod back interminably to extend line. That procedure only serves to disturb any trout in the target area.

Using the double-haul requires only one or two cycles of rod flexion with only a small portion of the fly line over the water. You can learn this at home while seated on the floor with only a fly rod tip and a short length of fly line, or even butcher cord, while working through the instructions laid out in front of you. Although you do need a little practice to master the procedure, it is extremely rewarding and deserving of the effort.

The Double-Haul

. . . .

This method of casting allows you to obtain phenomenal distance with a fly rod and line. My competitive record stands at 208 feet, achieved in the World Casting Championships at Oslo, Norway, in 1976.

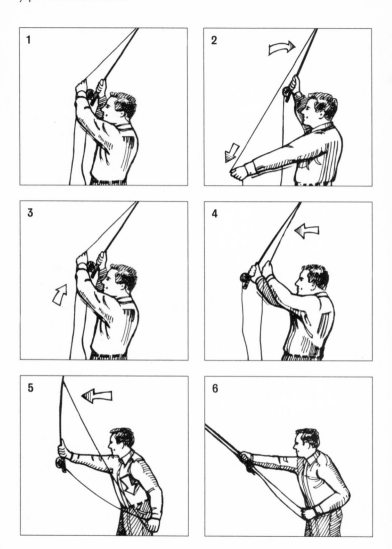

fig. 2: DOUBLE-HAUL CASTING

1. The rod is gripped firmly in the right hand; the left hand holds the line (see fig. 2, facing).

2. As the right hand passes the shoulder, taking the rod into the back cast, the left hand pulls the line downward. This loads (energizes) the rod.

3. The left hand rises immediately and feeds the line, without releasing its grip, into the guides to complete the back cast.

4. Then, when the rod loads, with the line loop straightening out behind, both hands (one gripping the line) and rod move forward simultaneously.

5. As the rod passes the shoulder, the left hand pulls sharply down again at the same time that the wrist turns the rod over out in front.

6. Line is released and fed into the guides at the last moment.

This technique develops tremendous line speed, maximizing the power in the rod and thus enabling the angler, by harnessing all its latent energy, to use lighter tackle yet achieve remarkable control and distance.

More Tips

. . . .

1. When you are false-casting, the rod should not travel forward beyond the 10:00 position and back farther than 1:00 (see fig. 3, overleaf).

2. The rod, line loop and casting hand should travel in a reasonably horizontal manner, never in a curve, with the rod's acceleration stopped dead at the moment the haul is executed, both front and back. There should be a slight drift of the rod backward, after the sharp stop, to allow the line to completely straighten before coming forward. Upon completion of the haul, the rod should follow the direction of the line as it straightens out and falls to allow for full line and leader extension.

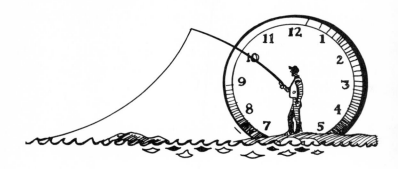

fig. 3: FALSE-CASTING

*The rod should not travel forward beyond 10:00
or back farther than 1:00.*

3. The rod should be treated as an extension of the forearm; therefore, the forearm must move in unison with the rod butt, the wrist breaking only slightly at the rear of the back stroke and, of course, when turning the rod over upon the delivery cast.

4. The later the line haul is executed in the casting stroke sequence, both in front and back, the smoother and more powerful the cast.

5. When practising the above to learn the double-haul, concentrate your visual attention on the hands and rod position and not on the line. This concentration will enable you to cast a tight loop, one with minimum air and wind resistance. A tight loop allows you to place the fly where you want it with little effort at virtually any distance.

Q: Okay, then. How many of you guys out there knew there was such a thing as competitive casting? I sure didn't, until I met the Old Guy. I have even had a career as a competitive caster, and pitiful it was. If you don't mind, I will tell you about it briefly, which might give you some insight into this strange world. This is a good time for a break—so say I in my role as editor/commentator—because Gordon is moving on to the subject of fly-tying.

*So what happened was, twenty-odd years ago I saw an ad in the newspaper: "*WANT TO BE A BETTER FISHERMAN?*" Well, I didn't want to be a better fisherman, necessarily, but I wanted to be a fisherman. I was at an odd time in my life. I knew, I intuited, that my life lacked passion. A passion, if you see what I mean. I more-or-less coasted along from day to day, doing a lot of things with no particular enthusiasm, save perhaps drinking and ingesting illicit substances.*

Somehow fishing came into my life.

How this came about isn't that important; the thing to

know is that I made this amazing discovery that when one
fishes, one is nothing other than a fisherman. It is impossible to step into a river, holding a fishing rod, as, say, what
I am today, a middle-aged midlist writer made miserable by
the collapse of his marriage. When one steps into a river,
one is an angler and one has only one problem, not a world
full. That problem is, simply, how to catch a fish, and all
those years ago I saw an ad where a guy was going to show
me how to do it better.

I went to a schoolhouse in Scarborough. There were perhaps twenty other people there, twenty guys who wanted
to be better fishermen. Gordon's recruiting strategy was
twofold. First, he gave a casting demonstration. He had his
then-wife hold out a peeled banana. Standing perhaps 40
feet away, he threw his fly line and sliced up the banana.
Then he took a tiny fly rod and demonstrated the double
haul, throwing the line the length of the gymnasium. At
least Gordon did this on his second attempt; the first time
he threw with the little rod, the line shot out, straightened
abruptly and fell to the floor. "It goes a lot farther," said
Gordon, pointing down at his feet, "when you're not standing on your running line."

Second, the Old Guy (he was younger then, of course)
took us into a classroom and showed a little 8-millimetre
film. The film showed him and his buddies taking speckled
trout out of a huge river in northern Quebec and, yes, here's
where I mention Fishing With My Old Guy, because
that's all about our adventures in that strange land.

I joined the club and came out to practise every week. I
had no real talent, but I had, yes, I had passion! I patiently
worked on my casting technique, throwing fly line tipped
with a piece of fluff at the targets set out on the gymnasium

floor. I learned how to bait-cast as well, tossing plastic plugs at targets with fire alarm bells in the middle; a bull's-eye resulted in a very satisfying ping!

In the summer months we practised at a little pool in the centre of a complex of office towers, the kind around which, during the day, secretaries sit and pull off their shoes and pick at their salads. We also took to the fields, practising the distance events. The distance games are—or at least look—the weirdest. The salmon rod, for example, is enormous, 17 feet long, as unwieldy as a caber. Throwing the game called spiderweb is a study in strange comportment. The caster holds a shortish rod (burdened with a tiny reel) and whirls like a dervish, whipping an arm with an enormous "ooph!" and hopping about on one foot to avoid stepping over the start line.

Gordon convinced me to go to the North American Championships, held that year in Cincinnati. We drove down in Gordon's land yacht. The Old Guy amused himself with the CB radio, identifying himself as Royal Coachman and asking about any traffic snarl-ups lying ahead.

Gordon himself had a rather good tournament, winning a couple of events. Then (and now, as of this writing) the dominant force in tournament casting is a man named Steve Rajeff, out of California. He won most of the games and was awarded the overall prize. I myself—and I feel duty bound to tell you this, because the tournament casters are meticulous record keepers—was pitiful. I did manage to get off one good shot, in the angler's fly, a distance game utilizing the double haul. I executed everything I had learned from the Old Guy. My line shot out splendidly— then it straightened abruptly and fell to the ground. I had been standing on my running line.

Fly-Tying
· · · · · · · ·

Other than tricking a brookie into believing that the little bits of flotsam and jetsam you toss out for its perusal are the real thing, perhaps creating your own trout flies is the most satisfying spinoff of the sport. Many folks practise the art of fly-tying but would never think of strapping on a pair of boots and offering their creations to an actual fish, just as some skeet shooters would never dream of firing their shotguns at a grouse or pheasant. To each his own, I say.

I began tying flies almost sixty years ago, after meeting my first fly-casting mentor, Dave Reddick. I concocted them from whatever I was able to scrounge from my mother's sewing box, clip from the family collie, or beg, borrow or steal from anywhere. On the bus on my way from school one day, a huge lady sat down in front of me, taking up almost the entire seat. I remember that although she wore a nondescript cloth coat, it was trimmed with an enormous flowing emu feather boa.

The temptation was irresistible. Checking to see if anyone else was looking at the mass of long feathers hanging over the back of her seat, almost in my lap, I surreptitiously whipped out my pocket knife and clipped off a couple of goodly sized clumps. They fitted in quite nicely with the potpourri of fur and feathers that comprised my fly-tying kit of the day.

I caught perch, rock bass and even a few pickerel on these early samples of my handiwork before I took my first brookie on a Brown Hackle, the most basic of recognized wet fly patterns and now the first pattern beginning fly-tiers in our club learn to tie. My father, seeing some of the creations and knowing my fascination with the pastime, bought me a wonderful oak tool-and-die cabinet. I know that I must have appeared perplexed until Dad said, "Go ahead, open it up, Gordon, and look inside."

The drawers were stuffed to overflowing with all the *proper* fly-tying material and equipment. As I write this, some fifty-four years later, I am still using the same case for my fly-tying gear and, amazingly, much of the original material as well.

The gift was for my sixteenth birthday, and I soon graduated into the next phase of fly-tying, assembling flies for the sake of the pastime alone. Under the tutelage of Dr. Carl Atwood, a renowned entomologist, trout fisherman and fly-tier, as well as instructor for the original Toronto Anglers and Hunters Association, I began tying a collection of all the well-known classic patterns, over 1,500 in all.

That labour of love, eventually filling several English leather fly books and celluloid boxes, took several years to complete. I did not fish with these, however, preferring even then to fish with fewer than a dozen patterns in a variety of sizes, depending on the fly. Meanwhile, the collection in the fancy Martin James fly books, for which I had scrimped and saved in order to house the flies in what I believed to be appropriate fashion, was trotted out on occasion only to show off to fellow fly-fishermen at sportsmen's shows and the like.

Alas, they and the beautiful leather fly books are no longer. They were in my possession for only a couple of years before I made the mistake of leaving them, along with all our tournament casting equipment, on the back seat of my buddy's convertible at a competition in Hartford, Connecticut. A thief, probably not even a fisherman, stole everything after slicing the car's roof open during the night while it was parked outside our motel.

Ever since that nauseating experience, my tying efforts, apart from one occasion, have been restricted to tying flies for fishing—and not show. The exception was in the fifties, when the president of the old Toronto Anglers and Hunters Association, Frank Kortright, asked if I would tie a set of a dozen of the best-known classic trout fly patterns. They were to be installed in a custom-made case and presented to the then Governor General of Canada, Viscount Alexander, on the occasion of his opening of the Toronto Sportsmen's Show. I still have and treasure the warm thank-you letter of acknowledgement that he sent me after receiving the gift.

> Q: It is true that tying flies can be very satisfying. It can also be a pain in the butt, as you clutch a piece of thread and a tiny bit of feather in your fat fingers and try to tie them onto the shank of a number 28 hook. Here's what I do. I set up my vice, take out my bobbin and all the material. I find a pattern and follow it carefully. Then I take my creation down to the shop and show it to the fellows there. "You see what I was trying to make?" I ask. "I want to buy some of them."

"Match the hatch." I have heard and read this statement ever since I first began fly-fishing for little brookies while tagging along with my Uncle Bob as a youngster. Although most fly-fishermen seem to believe that the suggestion is almost a biblical commandment, there is a tiny minority of us who have learned from experience that the size, general shape and manner in which the fly is fished are the real criteria for fly-fishing success.

In my early years with the long rods I soon came to the conclusion that although tying many kinds of complicated fly patterns was a pleasant hobby, it was completely unnecessary for catching trout. I soon developed a habit of carrying fewer than a dozen patterns with me on the stream and eventually reduced that number even further. In the last ten or fifteen

years, I have seldom carried more than a half-dozen patterns in
my kit. These are in order of customary usage:

1. The Peacock Despair (originated by Jack Sutton)
2. The Green Despair (also by Jack Sutton)
3. The Muddler Minnow (originated by Don Gapen)
4. The Muscarovitch (originated by Jimmie Stark)
5. The Brulé (originated by me)
6. The Adams (I suppose, by someone named Adams)

In the unlikely possibility that there is a fly-fisherman out
there who has never heard of matching the hatch, this expression simply means fishing with a fly that as closely as possible
resembles whatever insect happens to be prevalent in, on or
above the water. The Despairs, my favourite flies as I tie them,
lightly modified from their original pattern, resemble numerous stream and pond inhabitants such as the crane fly, stonefly
and dragonfly nymph.

The Despair, in both its versions, probably accounts for 80
per cent or more of the trout that I have taken on the fly rod.
And luckily for me it produced what is reputed to be the largest
brook trout ever caught on a fly, 29 inches long and weighing
in at 11¼ pounds. That huge brookie was caught in northern
Quebec's Broadback River and took almost an hour to bring to
heel in the fast water.

I fish the Despairs in sizes from 2 to 8, with 4s and 6s getting the nod most of the time. Here are the patterns with my
modifications:

The Despair
. . . .

The Despair fly, originally created by Jack Sutton in 1930, is, in
my opinion, the finest (in terms of catching fish) trout fly ever
created. In the fifty-odd years that I have been tying and using

this fly (fished like a nymph), many thousands of trout—brookies, browns and bows—have fallen to its charms.

Here are my versions of Mr. Sutton's wonderful trout fly for your use in tying. I use two basic versions, the original Peacock Despair and the newer Green Despair.

THE PEACOCK DESPAIR

Materials:
Thread
Number 2, 4 or 6 Sproat hooks
4-strand scarlet floss
Medium gold oval tinsel
Peacock herl
Bodkin or needle
Grouse wing or Hungarian partridge breast
Pheasant tail
Dark badger hackle

Wrap thread around middle of hook, then back to bend just before hook turns downward. Tie in 3 to 4 inches of twisted 4-strand floss for the ribbing. If preferred, tie in oval tinsel for ribbing instead of floss. Tie in four or five strands of Peacock herl. Wrap herl forward, leaving room at front for wing and hackle. Form a sparse tag with ribbing material before winding forward (well spaced).

Select two well-striped feathers for the wing. They should be just slightly longer than the hook shank. To facilitate positioning wing, flatten butts of the feathers after stripping excess by pressing them with scissors handle against table surface. Draw wing feathers firmly between thumb and bodkin to accentuate curve. Tie in wings flat and horizontally.

Select two pairs of pheasant tail fibres for legs. Tie overhand knot in each pair, positioning knot to about half the length of the hook (see fig. 4, overleaf). This is most easily accomplished by arranging fibres in a U shape between thumb and finger (step 1), then folding fibre tips back across the U to form a circle with the tips across it (2 and 3). Use bodkin or needle to pluck the tips through the circle (4), then pull tight slowly while positioning knot (knee) for length (5). Legs are tied in, one pair at a time, so that they resemble a swimming frog-legs action (6).

Select badger hackle so that fronds when extended just reach the barb tip. Tie in completely around throat. With thumb and first fingers of left hand, fold hackle back and tie over to form head.

THE GREEN DESPAIR

Exactly the same as the Peacock Despair, except the body consists of green seal fur with gold ribbing.

Fishing the Fly

. . . .

The Despair is a wet fly and fished as a nymph. Although there are trout that are foolish enough to mistake our feathered offerings for something edible, a fly that is worked and given a lifelike motion in the water will almost always entice more fish than one simply allowed to swim in a dead drift in the current. Imparting a natural appearance with a Despair is simple.

A hand-over-hand, or finger, retrieve of the line, simultaneously performed with a slight twitch of the rod tip, causes the wing and neck hackle feathers to open and close and the legs to swim in a manner that is not duplicated in any other trout fly that I have ever seen. The size of the fly is not as important as its silhouette and the way it is fished, although I am a firm believer in using larger flies on most occasions.

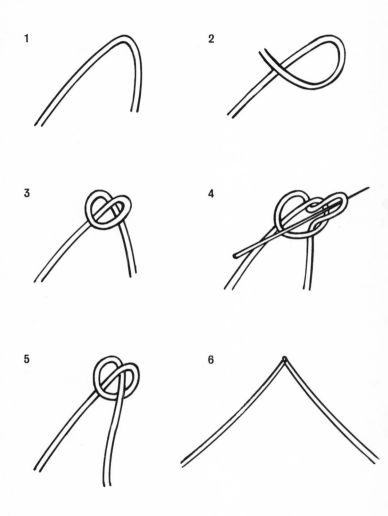

fig. 4: TYING DESPAIR LEGS

Many fly-fishermen, adhering to the "fish deep" philosophy, will tie their flies with a twist or two of fine lead wire to put them down where the big fellows lurk. Some even go so far as to crimp tiny split shot on their leaders to achieve the same result. If you have ever tried fly-casting with one of these weighted creations or leaders whistling by your ear, you must have pondered whether the risk to your person was worth it.

If you must use weight, may I offer a tip from one of my old fishing buddies? When he felt that he had to weight his flies because of the depth of the waters he was about to fish, he would cut lengths off the top wraps of wine bottles that he saved for this purpose. These were almost always made from a fine, leadlike sheeting material and served his purpose perfectly. Needless to say, he accumulated far more of the material than he was ever able to use himself.

I firmly believe, however, that a nonweighted fly swims in a far more natural manner than one with a lead anchor attached to its torso. I cannot imagine that there is an insect, or insect larva, that weighs as much as even a lightly weighted artificial trout fly—or swims in the same manner.

With the plethora of new high-density fly lines on the shelves nowadays, some of which are rated to dive to 30 feet almost instantaneously, and products that assist leaders to sink rapidly as well, I do not believe that there is any need to apply weight to the business end of your tackle to get the fly down to any required depth. My only concession is to use Sproat hooks for all my Despairs, as these hooks are formed from a slightly heavier wire than most.

Q: *There you go. As I said in the Introduction, you should probably dog-ear this section. The Despair is a wonderfully effective fly, and I know that because even I have caught*

fish on it. It's true that it's not much fun tying little knots in
pheasant tail fibres, but after a little practice, you'll be half-
blind and your fingers will ache and you will go down to
the tackle shop and buy the little buggers already made.

I disagree with the oft-expressed opinion that small trout flies do less damage to released fish than their larger brethren do. Number one, the larger flies are more easily gripped and removed, by simply pressing in the opposite direction of the barb; and number two, small flies are often inhaled completely, ending up in the trout's gills or throat, where the damage is irreversible.

The use of barbless hooks for the flies pretty well negates the problem, other than for deeply hooked catches, such as those that often occur with such an overwhelming enticement as a properly tied and fished Despair. Even when fly-fishing for pan-sized brookies in a tiny creek, I seldom tie on anything smaller than a size 6.

I have learned that the farther your fly is from the end of the fly line, the more interested the trout may be in investigating it more closely; thus, I use leaders as long as the conditions allow. If a trout approaches the fly from the front, the perspective creates the illusion that the fly is right on the front of the fly line, often spooking the potential catch.

This is an especially important consideration when you are fly-fishing in lakes where you must make long casts toward the shoreline cover. Under these circumstances I use leaders at least 15 feet long and occasionally as long as 20 feet. The brookies in the cover in this situation will be approaching the fly from the front as you begin your retrieve. Conversely, long leaders are an unnecessary nuisance on smaller waters such as brooks, streams and heavily weeded ponds.

Nymphs
. . . .

There are literally thousands of nymph patterns; entire books have been published on nymph trout flies alone. The bible for anyone wishing to research the subject completely is Ernest Schwiebert's colossal 1,100-page tome, appropriately, if not imaginatively, entitled, *Nymphs*.

I once cleaned a 6-pound rainbow trout that we caught in Sludge Lake (believe me, that is the real name of the lake) that had half a dozen of the largest caddis cases that I had ever seen, or even heard of, in its stomach. Every one of them was at least 4 inches long. After a couple of hours researching everything I could find in my own sparse collection of fishing literature, I called old buddy Jack Wilkings. He possessed a much more comprehensive library of books pertaining to angling than I, along with an extensive number of works dealing with trout flies and the various critters and larvae that they are meant to represent. It only took him a moment or two of browsing in Schwiebert's book to locate the description of this giant member of the caddis fly family, which houses its larvae in incredible cases fashioned from leaves that have drifted to the bottom of the lake. I still have several of these cases frozen in blocks of ice to show skeptics when I relate the story.

Most, if not all, nymph fly patterns are intended to resemble one or more of the larval stages of one kind of insect or another, such as stoneflies, mayflies, crane flies and so on. Any of these will catch fish—someplace, sometime, somehow—but so will a piece of fluff picked from the lint catcher in your clothes dryer. Once again, at the risk of sounding like a broken record, how a lure or fly is fished is the key to success.

About twenty years ago, Jack Wilkings invited Peter Poku-lok, Don Allen and me to join him for a three-day weekend of trout fishing at his cottage on Blue Lake in Quebec's Temis-camingue area. During that memorable weekend I caught the most trout I had ever caught in a three-day period: more than 150 brook and lake trout—*and all caught on flies!* The trout were so voracious that they would continue to attack our flies until the hooks were almost stripped bare of dressing. I would catch a dozen or more trout on my Despair, even if the legs were ripped off, the wing torn away and the peacock and ribbing reduced to tatters. The trout still attacked.

At the end of the first day, as Jack and I were cleaning up the kitchen and the other two were snoring away on the chester-field, Jack suggested that we try to tie some flies that the trout wouldn't hit. I told him that I'd been admiring the gorgeous shag carpeting he had all over his cottage—even in the bath-room. "You know, Jackson," I said, "that bright orange and yel-low tufting reminds me of a fly I fished with years ago, only it was black and yellow, a McGinty. Where can I clip a bit of this stuff off to tie something up with it?"

Thinking he might suggest that I look beneath the ches-terfield or something, I was startled when he replied with a mischievous grin, "Well, I've been planning to replace the bath-room carpeting that's around the toilet as it's rather badly stained. Take whatever you need from there."

After we got bored tying up the Shaggies, Jack tiptoed over to the chesterfield, where Pete and Don were still sound asleep, and proceeded to clip samples of hair from both their heads. Pete, however, woke up just as the little lock of hair was pur-loined from his scalp. His yelp woke Donnie up, too.

Once we explained our plan, they asked what we were going to contribute to the project. So Jack stripped off his shirt, while I lowered my pants and shorts for a little mutual pruning. Thus the infamous Ches-croch'n-ed streamer fly was born.

Once the newly collected samples were carefully placed in cellophane packages, Pete doffed his own shirt, raised his arm and said, "Help yourselves, gentlemen."

The next morning, the other fellows gave the Shaggies their trial by fire. The trout loved them. I decided to give the Ches-croch'n-ed a try.

The fish we had been catching off the dock were mostly lake trout in the 2- to 4-pound class that were cruising the shallow shoreline in search of a feed in the still ice-cold waters of early May. For every brookie that it surrenders, Blue Lake generally produces ten or so lake trout, but the Ches-croch'n-ed was about to reverse that ratio in favour of the specks.

Hoping to locate undisturbed fish, I decided to make my first cast much farther out than the in-shore areas that the other fellows had been working over. With a quick double-haul on the line, the ugly streamer sailed 90 feet out from the dock. The moment it struck the water, it was seized and a violent thrashing erupted on the surface. The fish sounded, tearing the remainder of the fly line off the reel along with 30 feet of backing before I was able to regain control.

"Hey, guys," I yelled, "this is a beaut! It's either a 10-pound lake trout or a 5-pound speck!"

I fought the fish for almost fifteen minutes before we could see what it actually was, a beautiful 4½-pound speckled trout. We still had been unable to find, or tie, a fly that the trout of Blue Lake would turn up their noses at. The payoff was that the Ches-croch'n-ed earned me fifteen bucks for the biggest brookie of the weekend.

Q: *It seems to me that anecdotes are an integral part of fishing. Fishing is about those times when exceptional things happen—such times raise the market value of our existences—and so the stories bear repetition. Perhaps some colouring, embellishment, but certainly repetition. Here's what I'm getting at. If a human being lived for a thousand years, angling would lose much of its value. Because one would certainly catch, at some point in that span, a 15-pound speckled trout. One would experience a freakish three-day feeding frenzy. There would be nothing but certainty and eventuality.*

But we don't have a thousand years, of course. We have our eighty-odd, so these events become rare and precious.

And so we tell such stories of wonder.

We speak of those things which our fleeting lives make look like magic.

With few exceptions, nymphs are far more productive than most other types of trout flies used for brookies. Many people believe that fly-fishing consists of using minuscule dry flies in an attempt to duplicate various types of floating insect life. This is definitely the classic impression fostered by many if not most fly-fishermen as well. But if you really want to put trout in your pan, you have to get down and usually deep to find your quarry. And that means, although it will be considered blasphemous in some quarters, using nymphs. We will look at dry-fly-fishing for specks at the end of this chapter.

Streamer Flies
. . . .

When nymphs (and I use Despairs most of the time) don't produce, there are several streamer fly patterns to which I resort. As with artificial nymphs, the manner in which you fish streamers—flies intended to mimic minnows—is probably more important than the pattern itself. In almost all situations streamers should be fished with a finger-pickup of the line interspersed with occasional twitches of the fly rod tip.

Even allowing the fly to simply rest and sink at times will produce strikes from inquisitive but cautious brookies. Anglers who keep in mind that a streamer fly should swim like a minnow, erratically one moment, at rest the next, or darting from one bit of rocky cover to the next, like sculpins, a staple in all trout diets, will achieve more success than the "cast it out and reel it in" fellows.

Books containing patterns for streamer flies, tied with feathered or hair wings, fill entire shelves in libraries. There are not only thousands of patterns but thousands of versions of each pattern, depending on the author-angler's own perception of the originator's actual pattern. But all hair wing and feathered wing streamers fall into one of two categories: those that depend on contrasting materials and general appearance and those whose materials are selected in order to create natural movement in the water on their own.

Streamer flies designed with a marabou feather wing fall into the latter category. Marabou can be long, fluffy ostrich or emu feathers or fronds from chickens with similar characteristics. They swim enticingly, like leeches, with little or no effort on the angler's part—an excellent choice for the lazy angler.

The problem with marabou streamers is that the wing is so soft that it often wraps itself around the hook shank and beneath the bend in such a way that it becomes unattractive to the trout. It also spins like a propeller in the air during false casting, creating a twisted mess of the leader tippet. For this reason, I suggest using shorter shank hooks for marabou streamers than for other streamer flies.

Hair wing streamer fly patterns are probably the most popular of all the flies used for trout, as well as for bass, pickerel and saltwater game fish. The hair used to fashion the wing can be polar bear, deer (bucktail), goat, squirrel or anything else that strikes your fancy, such as hair from the family pet.

Bucktail hair is hollow and therefore tends to float somewhat above the hook shank when at rest, whereas the stiffer polar bear hair tends to retain its position lying flat across the shank. Polar bear hair has another advantage over most hair wings in that it is shiny and slightly translucent, as are most of the minnows that streamer flies are supposed to be imitating. For best handling and appearance in the water, hair wing streamers should be constructed with the length of the wing only slightly longer than the hook itself.

Many of the most revered patterns were designed to suggest the lighter underbelly and darker back of a minnow, while others simply attempt to attract trout by using bright and contrasting colours. A few of the classics that continue to produce brookies for my friends and me are the Muddler Minnow, Royal Coachman, Parmachene Belle, Black Ghost, Leech and, of course, the well-known Mickey Finn. All of these can be tied in either feathered or hair wing patterns. The Muddler, Royal Coachman and Mickey Finn top my list of classic favourites. The Muddler Minnow, originally designed by Don Gapen to mimic the sculpin, a minnow that can be seen darting among the rocks on bottom in almost all trout waters, is a hybrid, a streamer with sections of both turkey tail feather and bucktail hair comprising the wing. The Muddler is number three on my list of all-time favourite flies.

The feathered wing streamers, tied in the classic style, use sections of either goose or turkey primary wing quills, which create a beautiful-looking fly, but one that requires impetus applied by the angler to impart a lifelike appearance to it in the water. As mentioned previously, this is easily achieved with a rolling-hand and finger-line-gathering motion in conjunction with erratic twitching of the rod tip itself.

I must state emphatically here that almost all streamer and bucktail flies are overdressed, or tied with overly generous amounts of material, both in the wing and on the body. There are only rare exceptions when a heavily dressed streamer will outfish a lean, businesslike version. Occasionally, I will pull out clippers and trim my own carefully tied flies if I deem them to be swimming unnaturally on the retrieve.

I do recall one instance, however, when a young fishing buddy of mine, Jurgen Brech, who had only been tying flies for a year or so, pulled out a huge Muddler from his box of goodies and tied it to his leader tippet. There was enough deer hair on that oversized Muddler to have made a shaving cream brush if he had wanted to. Never loath to speak my mind, I blurted out, "Heh, Jurg, you've got way too much deer hair on that thing. No self-respecting brook trout in this lake will ever give it a look-see."

I unhooked my clippers and passed them to him, saying, "Here, why don't you use these and trim it down to size."

"Thanks, Gord," he replied as he began to work line out in the air, "but I think I'll give it a try anyhow just like it is . . . if it's okay with you. All right?"

Of course, Murphy's Law, the exception that proves the rule, or whatever else you want to call it, then took hold of the moment. While I was changing my own fly, a beat-up Despair, for a rather scrawny Muddler Minnow, Jurgen, much to my chagrin, let out a war whoop and proceeded to play the largest brookie of the day to a standstill. He was enough of a gentleman to let me off the hook with only a smug smile and not a word of: "What was that you were saying?"

There are a couple of more modern streamer fly patterns

that have proven their worth on some of the biggest brookies in the world, the monster trout of northern Quebec's Broad-back River. On our annual safaris to this mother lode of giant brook trout, my buddies and I will occasionally put away the Despairs and Muddlers to give these other patterns a workout.

The alternates in our arsenal are the Muscarovitch and the Brulé. The former is a somewhat bastardized version of a streamer designed fifty years ago by Jim Stark, a well-known fly-fisherman and fly-tier. Jimmy's fly, which he named the McStarkovitch, was designed to appeal to the customers of the sporting goods store where he was the resident fly-fishing guru.

Although his fly caught fish, I felt it was unnecessarily overdressed, probably in an attempt to impress the store's customers. So we took the liberty of using his basic pattern but removed the tail along with some of the additional feathering that he had applied to the design. We could no longer use his name for the fly, so it became the Muscarovitch, a grey squirrel hair wing with a light overdressing of a few wisps of polar bear.

The effect created in the water, along its dark badger hackle and gold-ribbed orange nylon wool body, is of a cross between a golden shiner minnow and a large sculpin. The fly quickly became and has remained a key weapon in our personal arsenal for big trout, especially big brookies.

Thirty years ago, while fishing for lake trout shortly after the ice-out on Brulé Lake, Pete Pokulok, Donnie Allen and I discovered that the few fish we managed to catch were spitting up dozens of tiny perch, no more than a couple of inches long. Back in the cabin that evening, we concocted as reasonable a facsimile of the young perch as we could with our somewhat limited portable fly-tying kit.

The next morning we wolfed down our breakfast at heartburn speed, as we eagerly anticipated making a substantial dent in the trout population of Brulé Lake.

The three or four flies, which were quickly named Brulés, did not last too long, for the lakers attacked them ravenously. We fished until our arms ached, keeping only a few of the larger trout to cut into steaks and releasing at least several dozen carefully back into the swim. The Brulés continued to impress us on subsequent trips to fish for brook trout in larger waters, such as rivers or lakes. They also brought quite a few brown trout to heel (on the rare days when the Despairs were unproductive) in rivers like the Ganaraska.

The Brulé is actually a rather simple bucktail streamer. The body is a pale orange nylon wool ribbed with medium gold oval tinsel. The wing is fashioned from bucktail, dyed yellow with a greenish tinge. The fly does not have a hackle throat. The Brulé has proven its worth on all the trouts, as well as bass and pickerel. I had a day on the Pigeon River that I will never forget when I used up three or four of these baby-perch-like flies to catch twenty-seven muskies, albeit smallish specimens.

The only other streamers in my fur-and-feather arsenal are the Royal Coachman and Mickey Finn patterns. These venerable oldies seldom get taken out for a swim, as I prefer the more natural-looking patterns mentioned previously. They do look nice in my fly book though.

Before I move into a treatise of fishing with dry flies, I should mention that although I stated earlier in this chapter that I have no use for weighted flies, when one is stream fishing and using shorter leaders, it can be difficult to get nymphs or streamers down deep enough in some of the larger holes. The solution to that problem is to form a clay or mud ball around the fly (forget about casting it) and simply lob it into the pool. It ain't fly-fishing, but as the fly washes clean, a couple of twitches of the rod tip can produce an exciting flurry of action as the brookies in the area become convinced that they are witnessing the real thing emerging from the bottom ooze. I should also mention that I haven't used conventional wet flies for years, since I prefer to fish nymphs or streamers when I'm not fishing dries.

Dry Flies
. . . .

Some of the most wonderful moments in fishing occur when all the action is just below or on the surface of the water. This action usually signifies that there is a major hatch, such as stoneflies, mayflies, caddis or other forms of terrestrial insect life.

Fishing a dry fly in these conditions can become a frustrating experience for even the most experienced of fly-fishermen, as the trout—brookies, in particular—seem to easily differentiate between an almost perfect reproduction and the insects they are dining on. The size of the fly is the most important consideration; the general configuration is the second factor to take into account.

Exact duplication is unnecessary and irrelevant and may become a deterrent in some situations, since it is almost impossible to create an exact duplicate of a live insect that will move exactly as the insect does. One exception is the Adams dry fly, which, when fished with a subtle movement of the rod tip on the surface after remaining motionless for a few moments, comes as close to resembling a mosquito as one can get with fur and feather.

I tie the Adams in its original pattern, as well as one with a slight variation. The original has upright slate-grey duck primary wings and a grey fur body, while the variation is tied with a quill body and spent wings tied with grizzly hackle points.

The quill body can be tied from porcupine quill or a stripped grizzly hackle feather. Several long moose body hairs tied simultaneously also make a lifelike body. In either case—fur or quill—a slightly raised thorax should be tied in place immediately behind the wings.

This is my favourite dry fly for the few occasions that I am not fishing nymphs or streamers. Fashioned on number 12 or 14 fine-wire dry fly hooks and fished accordingly on a warm summer evening when the real things are driving you crazy can provide exciting action.

I use only two other dry flies, having decided long ago that it was more productive to fish properly with several winning patterns than to spend all those precious moments leafing through fly boxes and continually changing flies, hoping to come up with the right one for the day.

My other dry fly choices are the Royal Wulff and the Mashigami, both of which have produced big brookies for me on more than one occasion. These are big-water flies, for use in lakes, large rivers and even rapids. The Royal Wulff is a variation of the Royal Coachman, one of the all-time classics and still a favourite of many fine fly-fishermen. Whereas the original uses white duck primary wing tips for its upright wings, Lee Wulff's version employs white bucktail for the same purpose.

Wulff, one of the greatest fly-fishermen to have ever wet a line, discovered while fishing in turgid, fast-flowing rivers and rapids in the windy wilds of Labrador and northern Quebec that his favourite fly, the Royal Coachman, was difficult to keep upright on the surface. He decided that replacing the standard upright duck feather wings with coarse white bucktail, or with white deer body hair, tied in split fashion, along with a tail tied with a similar bunch of deer hair, would do the same job but in superior fashion.

He was correct. Because it is hollow, deer hair is buoyant and provided all the flotation Lee was seeking. He retained the peacock herl body of the original pattern, along with the scarlet floss ribbing and dark brown neck hackle. The pattern was suitably tabbed by others the Royal Wulff and in short order became a classic in its own right. I fish this pattern mostly in large sizes: 4s and 8s.

I have never been able to learn the identity of the lady or gentleman who originated the Mashigami dry fly. Suffice to say that I believe it was invented by a northern Ontario fishing guide, or perhaps by Dan Gapen himself. This, too, is a heavy-water pattern, most likely first fashioned for fishing the Nipigon River, the watershed that produced the long-lasting world record brook trout more than eighty-five years ago and where the Gapens, Don and Dan, spent most of their lives.

Like Lee Wulff's famous fly, the lesser-known Mashigami also uses the buoyancy of deer hair to keep it on the surface, only it employs the grey-brown natural hair rather than white. The body is also fashioned from clipped and spun deer body hair, densely tied in place before being trimmed into shape. This fly is so buoyant that it could probably keep an angler who fell into the river afloat long enough to reach shore safely.

Both the Royal Wulff and the Mashigami, also tied in larger-than-normal sizes, are fished with considerably greater motion than more conventional dry flies. Their bulk, along with the large amount of deer hair, creates an impression of a full-course meal thrashing on the surface to a big brookie observing the scene from its haunts in the depths.

Q: Hey there. I know it's been quite a while since I interrupted in my capacity as editor/commentator, but I have to admit to being a little out of my depth in these

discussions of fly patterns. I feel great kinship with that
angler who, when asked which was his favourite fly, replied,
"Some little brown thing."

There is one other classic pattern that has provided me with a couple of memories—the McGinty. It can be tied in either wet or dry fly fashion and is normally tied in small sizes on number 8 to 12 hooks.

The McGinty, meant to resemble a bee, does so only in so much as its body is tied with alternating black and yellow chenille rings. Conventional white duck primary segments form the wings, along with a couple of turns of dark brown hackle at the throat. When I was about twelve or thirteen and wanted to impress my girlfriend on a movie date, I hooked and caught a goldfish in the theatre lobby—on a McGinty.

I have no idea why I chose that fly, but having seen these big fantail goldfish swimming in a 6-foot-long aquarium on a previous date to the theatre (The Imperial in downtown Toronto), I had been planning the foolish scheme for quite a while. The fly was tied to a short length of leader, and the stunt was performed when the ushers in the lobby looked away for a moment.

As I hoisted the 6-inch goldfish from the tank, it spat out the McGinty and then flopped around on the floor. At that point my date left me, and I stood there foolishly trying to grab the slippery catch so that I could return it to the aquarium before it expired.

Luckily, I was not apprehended by the attendants, and eventually I sheepishly located my date in the dark theatre. It's beyond my comprehension, but for some reason or another she had failed to see either the humour or the challenge in the episode, and we never dated again.

Five years after my Imperial Theatre tour de force (or was it a debacle?) while helping my father as a stage assistant on the road version of his radio program, *The Fun Parade,* I was asked by the hosts of a banquet that was being organized for us by the local producers if I would like to do "a little trout fishing." This was in Charlottetown, Prince Edward Island, in the spring. They explained that they had arranged some sort of special dispensation, so that even though the season not quite open and I had no licence, I would be allowed to keep as many brook trout as I could catch in a two- or three-hour period.

"We need thirty or forty mudders, anyhow . . . for the banquet," they informed me.

In much of the Maritimes, brookies are referred to as mud trout, certainly apropos in PEI as the vividly red soil of the island stains most of the waterways an unsightly reddish-brown in springtime. The next morning I was driven to a delightful little stream, which, I was told, emptied into the Atlantic a few miles away; handed an old English split-cane fly rod and an assortment of wet flies with which to do battle; and told that they would be back in a couple of hours to pick me—and the fish—up.

Less than two hours later I had to call it quits, as there were at least three dozen smallish brookies, the largest about a pound, along with a 4-pound grilse (young Atlantic salmon) on the bank behind me in a washtub full of ice that had been provided for the exercise. The fly that did most of the damage on that memorable morning was the McGinty.

CHAPTER FIVE

Ice Fishing for Brookies

. . . .

Probably the least-known exercise practised in the pursuit of brook trout is ice fishing. When this sport is mentioned to non-aficionados, they almost always react with a grimace and derogatory remark such as, "I don't see how you can spend a whole day cooped up in those little huts staring at your bobber or whatever."

Or, "I guess it's a good excuse to get away for a day to do some serious drinking, eh?"

Well, my buddies and I, all trout fishermen, neither fish in a hut nor spend the day out on the ice drinking. As a matter of fact, we are virtually all nondrinkers. Of course we would rather be at the foot of a set of rapids tossing dry flies at brookies, or methodically working little brooks for a feed of these pan-sized beauties, but, in the middle of winter, when it comes down to either watching fishing shows on television or ice fishing, for us, anyhow, it is no contest.

We fish for brookies through the ice as often as we can in the winter months, beginning every year with the New Year's Day season opener. I have managed to participate in this particular season opener without a miss for more than forty years.

No New Year's Eve partying and frolicking for me. Attending this ritual is paramount in our annual angling scheme of things, so it is early to bed the night before, then up at 3:00 the next morning.

Fuelled with enough coffee to stay awake for the three-hour drive, we head north to one of the myriad brook trout lakes in southern Ontario, either in the Land O' Lakes area or the Haliburton Highlands. Many lakes in these areas are periodically stocked with brookies by the Ministry of Natural Resources, and many of these are easily accessed by automobile.

Although it is not necessarily always true, we adhere to the philosophy that the grass is always greener on the other side of the fence. Most of the lakes we fish are far enough off the road to ensure that only dedicated nuts like ourselves are willing to endure the travails of either hiking on snowshoes or wrestling our snowmobiles through deep snow—sometimes travelling as much as 7 or 9 miles—to reach them. After all, we reason, as with stream fishing, the less the traffic on the "hard water," the more receptive the brookies should be to our offerings.

Before I get too deeply into the methods we use in winter fishing, I must describe a method of ice fishing that was explained to us by a grizzled old fellow whom we met when we were just kids on our first ice-fishing trip out on Lake Simcoe. Seeing that my buddy and I had no perch on the ice, he asked if we would like to know how he fished for these tasty morsels. I replied, "Of course, Sir."

He explained, "Well, young man, all you really need is a good axe and a big can of peas."

We listened intently as he continued, "First you use the axe to cut yourself a two-foot-wide hole in the ice. Then you open the can of peas with the axe and spread them carefully on the ice all around the edge of the hole."

Pausing to see if we were paying attention, he continued in deadpan fashion, "Got it?"

When we nodded affirmatively and he could see that we were listening intently, he said, "Then, when the fish come up to have a *pea*, just hit 'em on the head with the back of your axe."

> Q: *You know, this is one of the areas where I part company with my Old Guy. I don't enjoy ice fishing. I've heard it said that it's better than no fishing at all, but I'm not sure I agree. No fishing at all is a lot warmer. I just don't think I'd enjoy getting up at three o'clock in the morning and driving up north and sitting out on the ice at minus-forty degrees and listening to that "pea" joke again.*

Our methods of hard-water fishing for brookies are not much more complicated than that old fellow's. But we have developed a set of guidelines that produce for us most of the time, even when the trout seem to have contracted lockjaw. Basically, we employ one of two systems: using live bait on a set line, or jigging with small artificial lures specifically designed for ice fishing.

We seldom fish farther than 15 or 20 feet from shore and sometimes, when there is an immediate drop-off, literally right up against it. Little depth is required; we set our lines in water as shallow as 18 inches and rarely more than 4 or 5 feet deep. We always try to locate an area close to good cover, such as near a beaver house, a fallen and underwater tree, rocky ledges or other such structure.

The Fish-O-Buzz
. . . .

Although brookies seldom wander far from their haunts, they do move around a little when the barometer rises sharply and can even be caught in the open, feeding on shoals well away from shore. Nevertheless, most of our brookies are caught in the shallows and within a few feet of the shoreline.

For centuries ice fishermen simply broke a supple branch off a shore-side bush, stuck it in the ice or a handful of snow beside the hole and fastened a length of baited line to the end of a stick or branch set to dangle over the hole. If they were lucky enough to be watching the branch (commonly referred to as a gad) when a trout took the bait, they would see the gad dip, and the race was on to see who could get to it first.

Fishing in ice huts brought necessary improvisations because of the limited space. These included a wide variety of what is known as a tip-up, a balanced stick on a small pedestal that would signal a hit by dipping or by rising should the fish move upward when striking, as in the case of whitefish feeding on the bottom. This setup still necessitated constant observation, or a strike could be discerned too late to set the hook.

For many years, before we came to the conclusion that it was a great deal more pleasant to fish out in the open on much smaller lakes for brookies, lakers and rainbows, I had an ice-fishing hut stationed out on the ice of Lake Simcoe every winter. Most of the time we caught fish in the hut but would return home with a blinding headache from staring at the tip-ups and attempting to interpret their every minute movement as a fish investigating our minnows.

One Christmas my younger daughter, Wendy, who was about a year and a half old, received a little toy plastic telephone as a gift from her granny. When she dialled an imaginary number, a spring inside would activate a tiny ringing bell. After a few days of listening to the continuous dialling and ringing of her phone, I could hardly wait until it was broken, as many such toys are shortly after Christmas. I was even tempted to hasten its demise but refrained from doing so in anticipation of its inevitable destruction, one way or another.

It only took a few days; when the dial stuck, Wendy had a bit of a temper tantrum and banged the little phone on the floor, breaking it into several irreparable sections. The sobbing quickly ceased while she consoled herself with her new teddy bear, allowing me to gather up the remnants of the wrecked toy phone. As I was about to deposit it in the trash bin, I noted the action of the dial and bell mechanism and—voilà—serendipity!

It suddenly occurred to me that the guts of the toy phone could somehow be used in an arrangement that would signal when a fish took the bait. Thus, the Fish-O-Buzz was born. It was a fairly simple exercise to rig up the original contraption so that a line suspended from a triggering extension would cause the clapper to ring the bell. Eureka—no more headaches from staring at the gads.

Although rather unsophisticated, the device worked well until we decided that it would work even better if the same principle was applied electronically so as to provide increased sensitivity to an investigative trout checking out the minnow. The resulting buzzer was marketed throughout Ontario and sold in the thousands.

When ice fishing for trout out in the open we use the Fish-O-Buzz, which consists of two hinged pieces of wood. The bottom serves as the support base, while the other upright section holds the buzzer and trigger mechanism. Powered by a D cell alkaline (because of the cold) battery, our buzzers can signal strikes no matter how sensitive and allow the trout to run free with the minnow. The result is usually an easy hookup and—most important—we do not have to keep our eyes focussed continuously on the buzzer, as we would have to do if we were fishing with gads.

Although emerald and silver shiners are the flashiest of the minnows, they are far from the hardiest. Our preference is for the more robust golden shiners when we can get them or, alternatively, lake chubs, with minnows of 2 to 3 inches producing the best results on most brook trout lakes. The hooks are placed either through the lips from bottom to top or just behind the dorsal fin. Care must be taken not to strike any bony parts, such as the minnow's skull or backbone, with the hook point. Worms, if they can be kept from freezing, will also take brookies through the ice and should be fished in exactly the same manner.

Wide-gap hooks with offset points in sizes 6 to 8 work most effectively when one is ice fishing for brookies with minnows. To keep the bait under control, we use a small flasher rather than a split shot or sinker; 1- to 1½-inch wobblers serve the purpose quite effectively. They should be tied to the line approximately a foot above the hook, with the smallest swivel you can find fastened to the bottom of the spoon to prevent the minnow from fouling up the short length of monofilament between it and the flasher.

This rig fulfills two other important functions. With the weight of the flasher pulling it down, line should be played out until it goes slack, at which point slightly more line than was used for the dropper with the hook and minnow should then be retrieved and a loop fastened over the tip of the gad or Fish-O-Buzz trigger wire. The procedure, done correctly, allows the minnow to swim and wiggle just off the bottom, where it is most visible and vulnerable.

On occasion the brookies are so voracious that little fuss is required to hook them. They simply attack and swallow without their customary predilection to play with the minnow or swim a few feet with it in their mouths before ejecting the bait, attacking once more, then gulping it down. Most often, however, the latter is the norm; therefore, patience is necessary. The trout should be allowed to swim well away with the bait before you set the hook with a sharp tug on the line.

Early in the hard-water season, with little snow and comparatively thin ice to cushion the sound of your footsteps, it is important to avoid running to the buzzer or gad when a brookie strikes. The vibrations from the heavy footsteps travel through the ice and water and are picked up by the fish, usually giving it second thoughts and frightening it away from your minnow.

Although most bait dealers package minnows in large plastic bags, which are given a shot of compressed oxygen (a fine way to keep them lively until fishing begins), we transfer them to an insulated cooler jug, which prevents the water from freezing while also keeping the bait in good condition. Rub the inside threaded portion of the lid with margarine to prevent the lid from freezing shut. The minnow net, too, should be kept in the jug along with the bait to keep it from freezing.

Ice fishing, in terms of excitement, has been compared to watching a bakery truck unload bread at the supermarket or watching paint dry, but the use of the buzzers does add a sorely needed element to the pastime. Whether you are grilling burgers over red-hot coals or sitting on stools alongside the Ski-Doo playing a game of chess, when the buzzer sounds off, summoning you from your reverie, it fires the adrenal glands into overtime.

It can have exactly the same effect on your dog if you take it out on the ice with you. Sadly, I have not owned a dog since my last Brittany spaniel, Jamie, died in my arms from congestive heart failure five years ago. He was the last of three consecutive, wonderful four-legged companions who used to accom-

pany me almost everywhere, whether it was in the field pointing and retrieving pheasants, quivering with anticipation in
duck blinds, as birds, barely out of range, flew by the decoys, or
running miles through the bush, following our snowmobile to
our favourite trout lakes.

Brittany spaniels are both pointing dogs and retrievers, but
their raison d'être seems to be to please their masters. Almost
everyone has heard about cats displaying their hunting
prowess by killing and dragging dead mice or birds home, but
how many folks have heard about a dog that retrieves trout? I
have been fortunate enough to have owned two who possessed
that unique capability.

My second Brittany, Trigger, would dive, even in fast water,
to grab rainbow trout and then paddle proudly back to shore to
display his catch. He did this a number of times in some of the
larger steelhead trout rivers flowing into Georgian Bay. If Trigger saw the hooked steelie jump, roll or splash on the surface,
he would leap in and perform what he considered to be his
duty, the retrieval of the trout.

I recall a day when, with the barometer falling, ice-fishing
action on A/B Lake was almost nonexistent. The big Brittany,
normally content to stay close to the fire on shore, became im-
patient and disappeared several times into the bush, probably
hoping to flush rabbits or a grouse. On one of his sorties he
was gone for quite awhile before eventually reappearing on the
opposite side of the lake. There were a couple of men fishing on
the point where he emerged after his hike. Within seconds we
could hear shouting and see them waving their fists furiously
at the dog, who was holding his head up proudly while trotting
back across the ice in our direction.

Their antics were all in vain though as Trigger, ignoring
them completely, carried the fat 20-inch brookie that he had

found back to his master. Puffing and muttering obscenities, the gentleman who had caught the trout had fire in his eyes when he eventually arrived where we were set up. His comments have no place in a book of this nature and are better left to the reader's imagination. Suffice it to say that pacifying the chap was not an easy task until I assured him, "My dog does have a 'soft mouth,' you know. That means he's been trained to hold his catch firmly without breaking the skin with his teeth, and there shouldn't be a single mark on your brookie."

An offer of a hot cup of tea was accepted and all seemed well, although after we returned the trout to its rightful owner, sipping his "cuppa," Trigger stared at him rather suspiciously and somewhat ominously. Within minutes, though, we were all enjoying a good laugh over the dog's performance. However, while the chap casually petted him, Trigger's eyes remained glued to the lovely speckled trout that the fellow was now loath to let go of.

That episode on A/B Lake has provided many a chuckle since, but a much more remarkable episode with my last Brittany, Jamie, occurred on another ice-fishing outing on the same lake.

It was a bitterly cold day with a gusting wind so powerful that most of the snow on the lake had been blown toward shore, leaving the ice so smooth it was almost impassable. We strapped sharply pointed creepers onto the bottoms of our boots to provide traction and help prevent a groin injury or, as happened to one of my buddies on the ice of A/B Lake one day, a broken ankle from a fall. Nevertheless, getting quickly to the buzzers when a fish bit still required a good measure of common sense.

Jamie, with his rather sharp and long nails, did not seem to have too much trouble getting around on the slippery surface.

He usually arrived at the buzzers before we could when they signalled the alarm.

Nevertheless, when he once had to negotiate a longer run because we were all clustered around the campfire trying to warm ourselves while cooking lunch, we almost beat him to the reverberating buzzer. But with a head of steam developed on the snowier surface near shore, he came sliding out past us, spread-eagled and looking exactly like Bambi on his first exposure to a frozen lake surface. As he slid by us toward the Fish-O-Buzz, his momentum carried him right into and through the setup. Sliding over the hole, his body somehow engaged the line, yanking it, along with a startled 2-pound brookie, up and out of the water and onto the ice.

When the dog and the fish finally came to rest—and seeing the hook protruding from the fish's upper lip—I pounced on the trout before Jamie could grab it and possibly become hooked himself. He has to be the only dog to have ever caught its own brook trout—and through the ice of a frozen lake!

Jigging
. . . . . .

When the buzzers remain silent for long periods, we jig, but jigging for brookies requires a great deal of patience. Whereas fishing with minnows and our buzzers allows us to pursue other activities and simply await the announcements that we have a trout investigating our bait, successful jigging usually necessitates continuing practice with little time for other activities. One never knows when a brookie might wander into the vicinity; therefore, the lure must be kept in reasonably constant motion.

The fellows I know that have the most success jigging, such as Rick Matusiak and my son, Randy, are rather industrious in their efforts and prefer to move to a new location if action is not readily forthcoming. I have seen them drill dozens of holes through the ice, trying to find a "hot spot." Other, more sedentary types, such as I, prefer to do our jigging sitting on a folding stool and remaining in one spot, normally a place that had proven fruitful during previous efforts, usually over a ledge or a drop-off near shore.

Jigging for speckled trout is best performed with a very short, relatively stiff rod and monofilament line that is no heavier than 6-pound test. Although I wrote emphatically about the general use of swivels on lures in most situations, as usual, there are exceptions that prove the rule. I already mentioned the use of a minuscule black swivel below the flasher on a buzzer rigging to prevent the minnow from twisting the dropper between the flasher and the hook.

The same tiny swivel should be incorporated into a jigging setup to prevent the lure from twisting the line. It should be tied into the mono at least 18 inches above the lure. The reason you can use swivels in these situations is that the line is not under constant tension, which would otherwise prevent their performing efficiently.

There are almost as many lures specifically designed for ice-fishing buffs as there are for summertime bass and pickerel fishermen. Many of the best come from Sweden, Norway and Finland, where ice fishing has been practised for centuries. Some of these, such as Normark's ice-fishing Rapala, are designed to swim in a circle with very little movement of the jigging rod. The potential width of the circle depends on the depth of the water and on how deep the lure is worked.

As in fishing a stream or lake in warmer weather, anglers who use their imagination and impart a little extra varying action to the lure usually produce the most strikes. Occasionally restricting the lure's circular movement to a barely quivering shudder can spur a curious but normally hesitant brookie to forgo its ingrained caution.

There is a wide range of sizes in this lure; the larger and heavier models are not necessarily intended for bigger trout but for fishing in deeper water. All sizes will produce brookies, the smallest working most efficiently in very shallow water; the others work best in greater depths. Because I do most of my ice fishing for brook trout in only a few feet of water, I jig with the smaller sizes when fishing with Rapalas.

Of the rest of the myriad lures that can be seen on tackle shop shelves in winter, a specially weighted and balanced wobbler with the unlikely name Swedish Pimple is the next most rewarding lure in my bag. Very tiny lead-head jigs decorated with a little Flashabou (silver streamers of Mylar) make up the rest.

The Swedish Pimple, if fished correctly, will swim off horizontally to the side, fluttering enticingly when the rod is raised with a sharp movement, then immediately lowered. The jigs seem to produce in a wide variety of actions, but bouncing them on the bottom is perhaps the most rewarding.

Another jigging method combines elements of both live-bait fishing and jigging and has proven to be extremely successful in certain lakes where for one reason or another my buddies and I fish for brookies in somewhat deeper water. With this method, we use the same flasher-dropper-minnow arrangement that is employed on the buzzer rigs, with two of the smallest minnows in the bait bucket, both hooked through the eyes to a number 6 short-shank hook. The motion of the jigging rod with this setup should be restricted to a subtle movement of the tip. A little observation will quickly demonstrate what is required to merely flutter the two minnows up and down near the bottom, while the flasher, barely moving, imparts additional vibrations throughout the water, helping to attract your quarry to the suspended bait offering.

It may not be as aesthetically pleasing as casting a hand-tied number 14 Royal Coachman dry fly over a feeding brookie at the foot of a waterfall in a spring-fed stream, or working the shoreline cover of a pristine lake with a silver wobbler, but hard-water trout fishing definitely has its place.

Whether you travel by snowmobile, snowshoes or shank's mare, or simply drive your car up to the shoreline, as can often be done in numerous southern Ontario areas, ice fishing for brook trout in the dead of winter is a great way to spend an enjoyable day in the outdoors. Furthermore, the trout you catch taste a heck of a lot better than breaded fishsticks from the freezer section of your local supermarket.

I will leave the last word on the subject to my old buddy Jack Wilkings, whose response when asked what he would do if he ever broke through the ice when ice fishing, was, "No problem! No problem at all. I would simply hold my breath until I sank to the bottom, pinch my nose, then run like hell until I reached shore."

Q: *Despite my stated distaste for ice fishing, the Old Guy is constantly after me, during the winter months, to accompany him on an outing. I demure, claiming family and work obligations. (This is, of course, bullshit. It's not that I don't truly have family and work obligations, what's bullshit is that such things would ever prevent a fellow from fishing.) I recall one time, however, when the Old Guy's badgering proved too much, and I agreed to an ice-fishing trek with him and young Paolo. Paolo is a large, good-natured young man, one of the ill-fated adventurers on that northern Quebec trip that I may have mentioned* earlier. *(Have you bought that book yet? In case you missed it, the title is* Fishing With My Old Guy.*) So plans were made: I was to be at Gordon's house in Scarborough at, I don't know, one o'clock in the morning or something godawful. But listening to the radio the evening before, I heard reports of terrible weather: strong winds, ice storms and temperatures in the minus fifties, such cold hell as could not be endured. So I phoned the Old Guy, and when the answering machine picked up I said, "Well, I guess we have to forget about it. I'll talk to you later."*

The weather reports were accurate, indeed, and I spent the next day inside, watching those heartbreaking television fishing shows.

The phone rang in the late afternoon. It was the Old Guy. "We missed you out there!"

"You went?"

"Sure, we went."

"Wasn't it, you know, terrible?"

"It was a little cold, yeah," the Old Guy adjudged. "It was worse for Paolo," he told me. "He didn't have a proper winter coat."

Brown Trout

CHAPTER ONE

The Reclusive & Elusive Brown Trout

· · · · · · · · ·

hen I was a youngster, brownies were often referred to as German brown trout, since they had been brought from Europe to stock North American streams. Now, referring to these challenging game fish as German browns is simply to give away one's age.

Browns adapted to their new surroundings in fine style, quickly spreading to waters all over the United States and in the southern areas of Canada, mostly through careful stocking programs but also of their own volition. Later they were introduced into lakes and rivers in South America, where they also thrived and reproduced prodigiously. Now they are found throughout the world wherever waters are cold enough to support the fishery—for example, in New Zealand, Russia and Patagonia.

Unlike their brookie cousins, browns are true trout. Although they often thrive in waters less pristine than those that support brook trout, like the brookies, they do prefer clean, clear, cold streams, rivers and lakes. But browns have grown to enormous size in waters that most humans would not dare to sip from on even the hottest day.

Artificial lakes and impoundments in many places, such as England and the United States, as well as the Great Lakes themselves, have proven to provide a veritable cornucopia of fishing thrills for anglers everywhere. These beautiful trout seem to be able to adapt to virtually any reasonable water conditions, providing the temperatures do not exceed 70°F.

Brown trout essentially feed on the same things that brookies find attractive, but the larger specimens have no qualms about helping themselves to some of the bigger inhabitants of their area. Frogs, crawfish, mice, moles, large minnows, suckers, ducklings and even their fellow trout often fall prey to big browns.

Although browns are generally thought to be mainly night feeders—and I believe that as they grow larger and older that rule of thumb does apply—many fine trout succumb to our offerings during the daylight hours as well. Nevertheless, as for most fishing, the morning and evening hours are normally the most productive.

These guidelines may not be applicable on big waters, such as lakes. For some reason, brownies residing in these waters seem to form their own dining hour preferences. These seldom vary within a lake but are not necessarily the same in one lake as in another.

Live-bait fishermen, spinning fishermen and fly-fishermen all take their share of brown trout, as do trollers fishing in the Great Lakes and many other large lakes by using downriggers while fishing for salmon and rainbow trout. A fishing buddy of mine and a fine member of our club, Rick Matusiak, regularly catches brownies over 20 pounds by simply fishing from shore in harbours at river mouths such as that of the Credit River, a few miles west of Toronto. Rick holds the Canadian record for the biggest brown ever caught on 8-pound line, a behemoth that almost bottomed the scales at 34 pounds.

Although I have pursued these lovely trout for over fifty years, the largest brownie to fall for my offerings weighed in at just over 6 pounds. I have had many opportunities to improve my record, but through a wide variety of unusual machinations and devious schemes employed by the fish themselves I have managed to release these leviathans to do battle with someone else on another day.

In *most* situations—in *most* places—during *most* times— brownies can *most* easily be lured out of their cover by an artfully presented spinner, worked with a spinning rod. Nevertheless, as in fishing for brookies, there are waters and times when aesthetically fly-fishing seems to be the only appropriate way to put fish in the creel and pan. Many places simply cry out for the use of fly gear, and dragging a worm or spinner through the water would almost be a desecration.

I know that in much of my writing an attitude of irreverence to the popular, almost religious, conception of fly-fishing might seem apparent in some quarters. However, most trout fishermen know one or more places that are just so lovely and rewarding to be in that there is no hurry to get a line in the water—being there simply seems to be reward enough!

In streams and rivers, where most fishermen seek them, brown trout could never be considered gregarious, preferring to spend most of their time holed up by themselves in deep cover. They seldom venture far from their homes, and it takes either a skilled presentation or a very lucky angler to bring a brownie out of its front door for a look-see at an offering. The bigger they get, the more cautious they become. After all, they did not achieve their senior citizen status by being imprudent in their choice of investigative sorties.

If you are successful in hooking, landing and carefully releasing a large brown, you can be reasonably certain that the fish will return to its same cover, providing you with not only the memory of the incident but an excellent chance for a return match with the big fellow—that is, if it is given a few weeks to regain its composure and lick its wounds.

Stories are legion about big brownies that have been hooked, released and caught several times during one or two seasons. While browns are generally not considered quite as succulent a table fare as brook trout, I have no qualms about keeping a couple for the pan, providing they were caught in a spring-water stream.

Like all freshwater fish, browns, either split or filleted, should only be cooked until the flesh loses it shine. To prevent over-cooking, fish or fillets longer than 9 inches should be lightly floured or dipped in egg wash, then coated with fine bread crumbs before they are fried in a little olive oil and margarine. For an additional taste treat, chop a handful of fresh dill into the bread crumbs before coating the fish. Fried over medium-low heat, the trout will be done when the coating browns.

Q: *When the Old Guy talks about cooking, prick up your ears. He is a very talented chef, and I agree with our pal Gary Benson (the fourth adventurer on my first excursion to northern Quebec), who judges Gordon to be the best outdoor cook in the world. Certainly some of the finest meals I've ever had were consumed in the extreme north of our country. Granted, I was usually in a state of near-starvation; still, Gordon knows his culinary stuff. There's more to come.*

CHAPTER TWO

Fishing for Browns with Live Bait

. . . .

As I stated previously, browns really do have a diversified appetite, feeding less often than their brookie cousins but often adopting the "gourmand" philosophy rather than the "gourmet." The best definition of the difference between a gourmet and a gourmand that I have heard is, "A gourmet is a lover of fine dining, while a gourmand is simply a glutton with a tuxedo!"

Moles and Mudpuppies
. . . .

Residing in my home freezer is a collection of interesting items removed from various good-sized brownies' stomachs during their obligatory autopsies. We always check to see what the trout have been feeding on. Perhaps the star of this "show-and-tell" exercise is a clear plastic container with five moles frozen in water. These were removed from a 24-inch brown that amazingly still had room for dessert and engulfed my Despair fly in one fell swoop.

Observing the brownie after it was landed and the Despair had been removed from its throat, I noticed two things: there was too much bleeding to release it, and the fish appeared to have some unusual malady that led to an extremely distended stomach. It wasn't until I was home a few hours later, after photographs were taken and the trout shown off to my wife, that the postmortem explained the brownie's bulging appearance.

Five of the moles (looking exactly like mice) were still in excellent condition, but a couple of others had already surrendered to the fish's stomach acids. They, too, were appropriately photographed alongside their captor, before being rinsed and frozen for posterity in the plastic container.

In another plastic container of ice in my freezer is an 11-inch-long mudpuppy, also removed from a 20-odd-inch brown. This archaic-looking bottom dweller, with its large, fleshy, fan-shaped gills, resembles some of the primeval characters in a Steven Spielberg movie, but in miniature. It is equally comfortable in or out of the water and has four legs, yet swims easily, using its eel-like tail for propulsion. The brownie that decided that the mudpuppy would make a fine meal obviously had no qualms about inhaling this diminutive fugitive from a Japanese horror movie yet still had sufficient appetite remaining to strike a number 3 Vibrax spinner. Some other unusual items I have removed from a brown's stomach include an 8-inch brookie, a huge frog and a crawfish big enough to pass for a small lobster.

An excellent time to go after big browns with live bait is during or after heavy rains that have swollen and partially muddied the stream, providing it still retains some semblance of visibility. Browns, however, like all trout, can track their prey with their excellent sense of smell, as well as with their sensory lateral line, which perceives and tracks vibrations in the water. Their olfactory glands can be seen on the upper jaw between the front of the mouth and the eyes.

With the water roiled up, the fish are less easily spooked and occasionally can even be found wandering well out of their cover in search of a meal or two, washed into the river from the eroding banks by the rain and runoff in the bush. The big brown that had made a banquet of the moles had obviously watched them being washed into the river when a stream bank collapsed after a heavy rain the day before. In similar situations I have taken browns that had absolutely gorged on worms, also washed into the stream by the rains.

Q: *Some of my favorite memories of fishing with the Old Guy involve brown trout. Not catching brown trout, exactly, but . . . well, here's what happens:*

We are in the heavy brush on the Ganaraska River. The river is to the right of us, and every few feet we will push through to the bank and judge our location. If there is a hole we can cast to, one of us will try. We take turns at the first shot. If it's the Old Guy's turn, I will sometimes let him go to the river alone—I'm often clumsy and afraid I'll spook the fish—and watch from a distance.

He walks to the bank, crouches slightly, spies a felled log across the small river. The Old Guy methodically lets out a length of line and, with a deft pendulum motion, lobs his lure. It comes within an inch of the log; the Old Guy has already begun his retrieve, working the Vibrax.

Suddenly the Old Guy grabs his heart and stumbles backward. He slips on the ground, falls to his keester. "Did you see that?" he demands breathlessly. "Did you see that brownie?" He holds up his hands, mutely trying to communicate great length. "It came out but didn't take. Did you see it?"

"Yeah, I saw it," I lie, not wanting to shatter the Old Guy's dumbfounded glee.

The Importance of Patience

. . . .

As a child, I was fortunate enough to have a wonderful uncle who would take me trout fishing with him whenever he could. Uncle Bob fished with live bait: worms, minnows, grasshoppers, crawfish, whatever. It didn't matter to him, as long as it wiggled, hopped or swam. The job of collecting the worms for him to use on the sorties when I was taken along fell to me. I considered it a fair price to pay for the privilege and learned much from him about fishing with live bait in the process, most of which is recorded in Chapter One of Part 1.

The main difference between fishing with live bait for brook trout and for brown trout is patience. My uncle taught me that in contrast to fishing for brookies, the secret in locating browns is to wait them out. With the brookies, if nothing happens when you fish a hole, you move on to the next one. Uncle Bob showed me that if you have a likely looking hole or bit of cover when fishing for browns, fish it until you are absolutely certain the hole is devoid of fish.

I remember fishing with him once on Cavan Creek when he suggested that I go on ahead and he would catch up with me in a little while. "Just wanna give this hole a good boo, Gordon. Saw a dandy here last week," he said.

Getting hungry three hours later, a couple miles upstream from my uncle and the backpack containing our sandwiches, I began working my way back to where I had left him, "just giving his hole a boo" for the brownie he had spotted earlier. He was still there, sitting on a stump and hiding behind a clump of streamside willows, while his fat dew worm drifted peacefully in a hole beneath the bank and under his feet.

Startled by my reappearance, he exclaimed, "Couldn't wait for me, eh, young fellow . . . gettin' hungry I suppose . . . right?

Didn't get a bite! Didn't see him, or any others for that matter either," he grumbled. "You know what that means, Gordon? That fish—and she's a big' un—is still there . . . probably resting . . . waiting for something different to come floating by for her dinner."

"I'm gonna get me a couple of big crabs (he called crawfish crabs) next week and come back and get her," he promised.

I remember another situation on the Credit River near the village of Cheltenham. I had been fishing the Credit quite often that summer and had come across a logjam piled up in a corner of the river where the 6-foot-high stream bank had collapsed, depositing huge blocks of clay into the jumble of logs. The whole thing created a perfect structure for a brown trout condominium. Although I never saw the fish, the fellow I was fishing with at the time, Ron Duncan, let out a yell and promptly fell back on his butt the moment his big streamer fly drifted into the only fishable opening in the logs below him.

"Oh my God," he muttered. "Did you see that sucker, Deval? At least thirty inches!"

"Yeah, sure, Dunc, but all I saw was the bulge on the surface of the water between the logs," I replied.

"It rolled beneath the fly but never touched it. That thing was longer than your hip boot, man."

"Yeah, Dunc, I believe you . . . but."

Of Mice and Men
. . . .

I gave that stretch of river another workout a short time later and was able to bring the big brown out of its cover once again, this time to examine a number 4 silver Mepps spinner, and once again it declined the presentation. Although the trout was visible for only a brief flashing pass beneath the spinner, I estimated it to be at least 10 and maybe more than 12 pounds, easily the largest stream trout of any kind that I had ever seen up to that time.

Shortly after that experience, I received a call from Ronnie Duncan. "Hey, Gord, do you get *Field and Stream?* There's an article you ought to see about big browns. This guy gets big browns, fishing after dark using white mice as bait. He floats them into place on a piece of shingle or something, then twitches them off when it drifts into the target area. Waddaya say we give this one a go on the Credit with that big guy up at Cheltenham?"

We bought two white mice in a pet shop, and a couple of nights later, wielding flashlights, trudged across several farm fields in our hip boots carrying spinning rods, pieces of cedar shingle and a little carton containing our secret weapons. Neither of us displayed any remorse for the potential fate of the tiny mice, with visions only of the huge brown resplendent on a varnished plaque or chunk of driftwood hanging on the wall in our recreation room alongside assorted brookies and bows.

After stumbling in the dark through unsuspected pitfalls, deadfalls and invisible wire fences, we approached the big corner pool where we poised to do battle. A toss of a coin, once the beam of the flashlight located it on the ground, would determine who would have first crack at the big brown. I lost the toss, but the task of rigging the mouse went to me, as Ron's hands were shaking like those of an old man plagued with Parkinson's disease.

The entire exercise would have made a great scene for a Laurel and Hardy movie. One of the mice escaped from the box when it was opened. We managed to fasten the other one to the little raft, but it broke free of the elastics before it could be floated into position in the dark when it snagged on the end of a log.

The problem was that we were keeping the flashlight beam away from the water so as not to needlessly alarm the trout.

When the clouds parted for a moment to reveal a bit of moonlight, we could see the little fellow quickly negotiate a foot or so of water, climb out on a log, shake itself like a puppy, then scoot away and out of sight in an instant. We made a few useless casts with spinners, but we both knew that we had blown the opportunity—if indeed there ever had been one.

I remember getting back there one more time, but it was not until the next year, well into the summer. This time, armed with only my spinning rod, I came around the bend in the river only to see an elderly gentleman well entrenched in the willows above the corner pool. He had even carted a folding canvas chair all the way into the river. With an enormous pack on the ground beside him, he gave the impression that he was planning on staying there for the duration of the summer.

Obviously, he's seen or knows about the big brown in the logjam, I thought.

I knew he had heard me approach, so—quietly and from a few feet behind so as not to overly disturb him while respecting his right as the first to be there—I asked him if he fished there often.

Half expecting his reply, I was still somewhat surprised when he replied, "I've been fishing here all summer, kiddo! There's a fish in here big as you. Had it on twice . . . broke my line once and hung me up on the bloody logs the next time."

"I've got twenty-pound line on now," he continued, seemingly glad to have somebody to tell his story to. "Been here since daybreak. You just gotta have patience and wait, wait, wait. Just been feeding the goddamn suckers all day this time, though."

He reeled in to rebait his huge Double Buffalo Muskie spoon with at least three large dew worms draped onto the barbs of the big lure's treble hook. When asked, he insisted that the concoction he was attempting to plop between the logs with his ancient bait-casting outfit was exactly what was required to get the monster out of its lair and up onto the bank.

"Damn near did it a couple of times, you know," he added.

The mouse experience was put on a shelf in the back of my mind until many years later when another fishing buddy, Gary Benson, and I had a similar venture on the Ganaraska River.

Although an angler wishing to achieve success on most outings should observe the general rules and guidelines laid down since the days of Izaak Walton and countless other experienced and skillful anglers, there are exceptions to everything. One of the cardinal rules is keep your fly or lure in the water as much as possible. Accordingly, we are not easily deterred from fishing, even though the Ganaraska River trout tend to run on the small side. The exception in this case could be the trout of your dreams, one that had never read old Izaak's book, *The Compleat Angler.*

Certainly one of those exceptions was a big brownie that sailed out from beneath an enormous willow tree that had fallen prey to the spring floods and toppled into a deep corner pool. It inhaled my Despair before retreating into its lair beneath the heavy cover. Although I could feel the movement of the brute below the branches as it showed off the Despair to its fellow trout, it was much too big and powerful for me to extricate, or even budge.

I applied as much force as I thought the 5-pound leader tippet could withstand while at the same time twanging the line and sharply striking the rod butt to transmit vibrations down the line. It is an ancient trick that will sometimes intrigue the fish into moving out of its cover to investigate the unusual sensations being delivered to it through the rod, line and leader. Although this little ploy occasionally does work, it did not that time. The leader tippet eventually parted.

I was fishing with Gary Benson that morning and he, wanting to increase his chances of catching a couple for the pan, had brought his ultralight spinning equipment along instead of the long rod. When I stripped in the line and discovered the fly missing, Gary asked if I was going to tie on a new one and have another go at the brownie.

Feeling that it would have been a futile exercise, I thanked him for his courtesy and patience, then suggested that the only way that fish would strike something else while it was already sporting a size 4 hook in its jaw would be if it was oddly different and much bigger than the customary fare it was used to seeing.

"Got anything like that with you that fits the bill, Gare?" I asked.

Because he also used it to carry a drink and his lunch, he happened to be toting his tackle backpack in addition to the fishing vest we normally wear, with its six hundred pockets—where you can locate just about anything, except what you happen to be searching for. The knapsack contained an assortment of tackle for larger game than trout, spoons and plugs designed for bass, pike and pickerel.

He replied, "I think I just might be able to find something in here that could do the trick, Gord. Let's have a look-see, eh?"

He took the knapsack off his back, removed his vest and spread it on a patch of grass, then proceeded to empty the pack of lures, one at a time, for our perusal. We narrowed them down to a couple that I liked but settled for Gary's preference, a number 11 silver floating Rapala, a big plug, 6 or 7 inches long, with an enticing action.

Because the plug was a floating model, I asked, "How will you get it down, Gare?"

"Easy," he replied.

Then, pulling a foot or so of spinning line out of his pocket, he held it and said, "I snagged it off the bottom in another pool."

Pointing to the row of lead split shot tightly crimped on the heavy monofilament, he continued, "This ought to get it down pretty good, eh?"

"Probably from one of the 'snagger's' outfits," he added while stripping off the weights and fastening them well up the line above the Rapala so as not to overly impede the action of the balsa lure.

He lobbed the big plug upriver and outside the branches extending across most of the stream. Then we both studied it intently as the current carried it, wiggling, into the depths, where we assumed the big fellow lay sulking with my fly in his jaw. Just as the lure came into view, the trout emerged from the hole, rolled over the plug and then, a second later, went beneath it. Luckily (for the brownie, that is) it managed both times to avoid the Rapala's hooks.

I used the adverb "luckily," but in reality I believe that the brownie was either just teasing us or simply taking a closer look at the offering before deciding whether it was edible or not. A trout does not grow that large by being irresolute. It must be decisive or fall prey to one of the many offerings that come its way—with barbed hooks on them.

Our brownie smartly refused to show again, even though Gary subsequently ran the gamut of big spoons and plugs in his possession. He even lobbed a huge Musky plug at the hole, almost breaking the tiny ultralight rod in the process. Probably an entire hour passed before we admitted defeat and moved on upstream. The rest of that outing was insignificant, but a different plan of attack on the big fellow was already formulating in the back of my mind.

I knew that the big browns of the Ganaraska River love to make a meal out of the moles and mice that often tumble into the water when the riverbanks erode after heavy rainstorms.

A few days later I bought a couple of tiny mice in a pet shop and headed back to the tobacco fields and the corner willow tree hole, which I hoped still contained the big brown. Feeling somewhat guilty at the planned subterfuge, I remembered that old Izaak Walton himself was not averse to using live bait when his artificial flies failed to produce.

I had already decided to make a sacrificial offering of the first mouse. My plan was to toss the little critter into the current in the same spot where Gare had cast the big Rapala, in the hopes that it would achieve the same drift right by the hole but, of course, on the surface rather than sinking like the weighted plug.

My reasoning was that with a trout's excellent peripheral and vertical cone of vision, if the fish were still there, it would see the mouse as it drifted by. Either its curiosity would be piqued and its appetite whetted, or it would ignore the offering completely.

I thought that it might possibly snatch the sample from the surface before returning for a second mouse, this one rigged with a small treble hook—or it just might examine the first mouse as it drifted by, allowing it to escape. If that were to happen, when the second mouse, weighted slightly, entered its front door, it would be considered an easy meal.

I searched for a small piece of driftwood, carefully attached the treble on my 6-pound line to the mouse with a firm elastic, then fastened the bait to the driftwood with another, but weaker, elastic. The plan was to position myself above the hole, toss in the free mouse, wait a few minutes (if my patience lasted), then set the second mouse adrift on the piece of wood in such a manner that, hopefully, the current would carry it safely by the branches to the front of the deepest section of water, where I would twitch it off the plank to allow it to sink into the big brownie's dining room.

I had envisioned this almost from the moment when Gary's Rapala seemed to excite the trout, even though it had just been hooked and escaped with my fly buried in its lip. It seemed like a rather grand and complicated scheme, just to catch a fish, but in reality was more like a challenging game or experiment.

The initial tease offer drifted untouched right by the tree, and the tiny mouse luckily made it to shore and escaped. Part two of the plan was then put in motion, with the rigged mouse on course as intended, until I applied the necessary twitch to free it from the driftwood.

I do not remember (possibly it was J. D. Salinger) who said, "The best made plans of mice and men . . . ," but the quote immediately comes to mind now while I am writing this little story and recalling the details.

Instead of the mouse's being freed from the float at the first twitch of my rod tip as planned, I had to exert a sharper pull to release it from the driftwood before it sailed too far. For some reason the wrong elastic parted and the second mouse, swimming furiously toward shore, also escaped its pre-ordained fate. That was the last time that I went to the expense and frustration of trying to fish with live mice as bait.

Q: We are talking about patience.

(Oh, of course it wasn't Salinger, I don't even know why the name Salinger occurred to Gordon. It's from a poem by Robert Burns, "To a Mouse." And the plans are "laid," not "made," and in fact they are "schemes," but none of that really matters, I suppose.)

No, we are talking about patience. The Old Guy has even cleverly forced us, by way of example, to summon our own patience. He did this by telling not one, but two stories, twice, within the last few pages.

Many people claim that fisherfolk need, possess, patience. The gentleman sitting in his fold-up certainly seemed to have patience. The Old Guy's dogged pursuit of big brownies seems to indicate patience.

But it's not true. Anglers don't possess any patience whatsover. But they are always willing to wait just one more moment. Over and over and over again. It looks the same as patience, but believe me, the feeling inside is a world away.

Grubs and Maggots

. . . .

Although I have many exciting recollections of fishing trips, most do not involve trophy-sized trout but rather revolve around unusual situations. I'm sure this is true for most anglers. According to my publishers, however, it is the trophy fish that the average chap contemplating the purchase of a fishing book looks forward to reading about.

Another live-bait memory easily recalled from my memory bank is of a fishing trip I took with my son, Randy. One of the biggest brown trout that I have ever had the pleasure of attracting from its haunts inhabited a rather inconspicuous corner undercut bank, a stone's throw from a bridge crossing the Ganaraska River. I have no way of knowing how many other fishermen knew about this fellow, but this brownie was an exception in more ways than one. It often hung out in the open outside its cover in broad daylight. I suppose its great size gave it a feeling of invulnerability. Yet even though the fish dwelled in a place on the Ganny fished by dozens of other fishermen during an average season, it continued its existence in the same place for at least several years.

There was no doubt in my mind that we saw the same fish each time, as the scars and torn lower lip from its battles were easily recognizable. The first time Randy and I saw this veritable Moby Dick of troutdom, in somewhat murky water after a heavy shower, our initial reaction was that it had to be either a carp or a freak holdover from the last chinook salmon run.

But carp do not exist in the ice-cold water of headwater trout streams, and it had been six months since the last salmon run in the Ganny. Nevertheless, Randy made a cast a few feet upstream from its nose. During the resultant explosion, when the fish simply disappeared from sight, we were briefly able to distinguish the gorgeous oversized red and brown spots that decorated its flanks. A trophy brown of at least 10 pounds!

We left the hole alone, hoping to put the fish at ease for another bid a little later (and to settle our own nerves), then continued upstream. A couple of hours passed uneventfully before we returned to the corner hole near the bridge. The water had cleared, and it was a simple matter to deduce that the big brownie made the undercut corner hole its personal retreat.

We flailed the water unmercifully for another good hour, all to no avail, before surrendering to the fates of that particular morning on the Ganny. At least, we thought, we will have the picture of that huge brown trout indelibly etched in our memory bank forever.

The story does not end there, though. Over the next couple of fishing seasons, my son and I provoked the big fellow into striking our lures several times; once he tore into my Despair fly, even though he was sunning himself right out in the open. That could not be considered a struggle, however; the fish just powered its way 30 or 40 feet upstream, then abruptly turned tail and charged right back down past where I stood, shaking like a leaf, and disappeared under the bank.

It all happened so quickly that the hook was never properly set in its huge jaw and the fly simply dropped out with all the slack produced by the trout's sudden return downriver. Reluctant to admit defeat once again, I began to think that just maybe the big fellow could be tempted into snacking on something a little juicier than my Despair.

Concealing my spinning outfit under a fallen willow, I took a plastic bag from one of the hundreds of pockets in my fishing vest and began a search in the cattle field adjacent to the creek to see what I could locate. An hour later, sweat washing the Muskol insect repellent down off my forehead and into my eyes, I worked my way back across the field toward the stream. I had managed to collect only a few grasshoppers, a brown locust and a tiny leopard frog.

As I neared the stream I could see a chap carrying a spinning rod coming across the field in my direction after emerging from the bush.

"G'day," he said, greeting me with a smile. "Just gettin' started? I saw you trying to catch hoppers. Did you ever try grubs or maggots for bait? They work great sometimes when nothing else seems to do the trick . . . especially for big browns."

"Looks like you're fishing with worms," I said. "Where in hell would you find stuff like that around here?"

"Easy," he said. "There's a couple of places I know of, anyhow. Got a sharp pocketknife? Come over here and watch this. See these lumps on the milkweed stalk? Sometimes you'll find a great little grub inside them if you're lucky. The trout just love 'em!"

Using my knife, he cut open several of the milkweed stalk lumps but failed to find anything.

"Like I said," he reiterated, "you don't always find the critters . . . I guess it depends on the season."

"But look over there," he continued, pointing to a freshly deposited and still steaming cow pie. "You can find goodies in these, too, sometimes."

Picking up a stick, he announced, "Let's have a look, shall we?"

Holding up my bag of grasshoppers and frog while glancing at my watch, I said, "I think I'll pass on that one, if you don't mind. I haven't got a lot of time, so I think I'll just give these guys a boo and see what happens. Okay?"

Before he could object I thanked him, wished him luck and promised to try his suggestions on my next trip to the river.

An hour or so later, after drowning the last of my hoppers and frogs—and only producing a couple of large chub for the effort—a peek behind me in the direction of the cattle pasture showed that the other chap had moved on downstream, well beyond where I was fishing. I thought that at one point the big brown that had been tantalizing Randy and me for more than a year had stuck his nose out briefly for a look at one of the hoppers.

The field beckoned, once again. Cow flaps, cow pies, whatever term you want to apply to cattle manure, it's still just a big pile of poop. But the idea that there might be a fat, juicy grub there for the taking overcame my revulsion at collecting the morsels from the manure. Although there were ample deposits to choose from in the pasture, it seemed logical that for grubs to be present and large enough for my purpose, the day-old stools would probably offer better results. A big stick was put to use, and several pies later, there they were—not large grubs, but a nest of large, teeming maggots, probably deerfly or horsefly progeny.

I realize that reading about grubs and maggots in cow pies is probably extremely distasteful for some folks perusing these pages. But it is a simple matter for the squeamish to skip this section. Nevertheless, as most fishermen have heard or read at one time or another about the use of these as live bait, it is appropriate that it be included here.

There also is an incredible tale that has mirthfully been propagated by mischievous anglers for centuries, dating back to the Izaak Walton era. Legend has it that maggots used for bait must be kept warm so that they wiggle and squirm, and therefore they should be kept in the hollow of your cheek until being placed on the hook. Just collecting the creatures was disgusting enough, however, so a plastic bag in the pocket of my sun-drenched fishing vest had to suffice.

Folks who have managed to avoid becoming nauseated reading this chapter so far probably expect to learn that we finally did catch the big Ganny brown. Well, the maggots did produce results. In short order I caught and released two small brownies, several chubs and a 14-inch rainbow, which was kept for the pan, but the real object of our labours could not be tempted to sample our wiggling wares.

> Q: *Fishing gets best when it gets personal. It's nice when a fish shoots out from underneath a log. It's better when the fish does the same thing, finally lured from its lair after long hours, weeks, even months of enticement. I recommend that you read William Humphrey's fine little book,* My Moby Dick. *I don't know why I'm recommending it, however, seeing as I know full well that none of you have gone out and purchased* Fishing With My Old Guy *yet.*

Worms

. . . . . .

Although many skilled anglers use live bait in their pursuit of big trout, other than ice fishing in winter, when we often use minnows, my fishing buddies and I prefer to fish with artificial lures or flies and seldom employ live bait. There have been a few occasions when I fished with worms, such as trolling in midsummer, fastening them to a leader and hook tagging along in the wake of a big gang-troll (a series of large attractor-type spinners on wire links).

Nevertheless, I do have another story about fishing with worms for big browns that deserves a few lines. There is a rather inconspicuous little stream called Sheldon Creek that winds its way for the most part through a number of farm fields, eventually emptying into one of the most popular trout watersheds in Ontario, the Nottawasaga River.

Only an hour's drive or so from Toronto, Sheldon Creek drains through potato and tobacco fields, occasionally meandering through the odd cedar swamp or dense bush. A trout angler observing this stream for the first time would be inclined to hike back to his car and search for more likely looking waters.

Back in the sixties, soon after I had begun marketing a lure scent called O'Fishol, I received an urgent call from a gentleman who claimed he had bought the entire remaining stock, about a dozen and a half pressurized cans, from Jesse Magder's popular Sportcam Sporting Goods store. Jesse had already turned over five or six cases of O'Fishol during the first couple of weeks of the trout season.

Unfortunately, although I do not remember the gentleman's name, I will never forget that phone call and subsequent discussions with him. The fellow had quite a story to tell—and he had the photos to back it up. He claimed that he and his two brothers had discovered the mother lode of brown trout glory holes and, even more important, had learned how to catch these fish with remarkable consistency.

Although many retail dealers are reluctant to purchase products from jobbers or wholesalers who sell their merchandise directly to the consumer, he pleaded his case with me so successfully that I agreed to sell him six dozen cans of O'Fishol for his and his brothers' own use, exclusively, on the provision that he never mention to any other fishermen or sport stores or to Jesse Magder that he had been able to obtain the lure scent directly from me.

He had asked if he could possibly get the cans from me right away. "I'll pay you in cash and it'll save you the shipping costs," he shrewdly added.

An hour later, when he arrived at my home to pick up the cartons, I insisted that before we close the deal he would have to elaborate on his explanation of why he needed so much of the lure scent.

"Take a look at these, Gord," he said, passing me a handful of pictures. Most had obviously been shot at night with a flash camera, but a few of the sharper photos appeared to have been taken first thing in the morning. There were pictures of him and his brothers in various poses around the remnants of a campfire on a muddy bank of a small stream, with a railway bridge in the background. There were beer cans and what appeared to be cigar butts scattered about.

I counted at least seven huge brown trout that would have weighed 5 to 10 pounds each stretched out on the bank for the photos, and the men were hoisting a couple that seemed to be even larger.

"One of those went almost twelve pounds," he confirmed, "the other, just over ten."

The photos and subsequent fish story (obviously true) were mind-boggling, to say the least.

Sitting on our veranda, cup of coffee in hand, he explained, "My brothers and I always fish with live bait, especially for trout. Last fall we were fishing the fall run of steelheads (rainbow trout) on the Nottawasaga River near Alliston when we decided to give this stream flowing into it a look-see. I think it's called Sheldon Creek."

He interrupted his story to ask, "Do you fish up that way, yourself?"

"Not very often," I replied. "My buddies and I prefer the streams east of Toronto rather than up there, but we do give some of them up there a boo, now and then."

"Ever fish Sheldon?" he inquired.

"Can't say for sure if we have," I answered, "but by the looks of it we sure as hell will be, soon."

Unlike 95 per cent of fishermen, the chap seemed not the least bit reluctant to divulge the facts about and location of his most unusual discovery, especially after I substituted a brew for his empty coffee cup.

"Well, one of the guys had picked up a couple of cans of your O'Fishol from Jesse's shop," he continued, "and we were soaking our roe bags and worms with the stuff like crazy when we discovered that it really did work. The three of us almost always have a stogie on the go when we're fishing. Keeps the bugs away, you know. I guess, like it says on the can, though, the stuff disguises the smell of the butts. I know we had trouble catching bows until we got hold of the O'Fishol.

"I remember one time I got halfway up to Georgian Bay to fish the Beaver River when I realized I'd forgotten the stuff. You probably won't believe me, but I turned around, drove all the way home and headed back up north after breakfast."

Carrying on where he had interrupted himself, he said, "On that day we found ourselves branching up the little stream off the Notty, we had taken a couple of five- or six-pounders and missed a couple of big beauts when we came across this deep pool half under a railway bridge. It looked like a good spot to take a break and eat our lunch, so we cut a couple of branches and stuck them in the mud so that they would support our rods, while our lines baited with worms soaked in the O'Fishol drifted around the pool.

"Got another beer?" Putting down the pictures I had been shuffling over and over, I said, "You're damned right I do . . . just don't lose your place in your story till I get back."

Opening the beer, he continued, "Well, there was nothing doing there and it really was pretty unpretentious looking compared to where we were fishing earlier, the Nottawasaga, but when we finished eating and reeled in the lines my brother turned red in the face and pointed at the big shape in the water coasting behind his hook. Don't know why, but he'd baited it with three worms and pretty well drowned them in your stuff.

"We could all see it. A huge brown trout! The biggest any of us had ever seen . . . but the bugger wouldn't take the bait, even when he let it drift back down to the bottom. It probably saw us and spooked."

I interrupted the soliloquy to say, "Browns like that seldom feed during the day, you know. Their dining habits become strictly nocturnal."

"Yeah," he agreed, "we found that out a couple of nights later. One of the guys had theorized that if the lure scent stuff worked on the rainbows, then it should work on the brownies, too, so we doused the bait bucket and moss where we store them with it. Then when we baited up the hooks with gobs of fat dew worms, we literally soaked them in it, too."

Glancing at his watch, he pulled out his car keys and got up, swearing, "Sheeeeeeit! I'm later than all hell! Gonna have to fight the traffic all the way home now. Can I get the O'Fishol now, please?"

Handing him his photos, I said, "They're downstairs . . . I'll get them for you right away, but I gotta know—" waving the pictures, I asked: "Is that really where all these were caught?"

"Yessirree!" he replied, emphatically, "last fall and this spring, night fishin' and all in the same spot. Now, I'm outa here. Okay!"

Even though I had seen the photos and he had just handed over two hundred dollars for six cartons of O'Fishol, I still found the whole story hard to believe. A few minutes after he left, I was on the phone to fishing buddy Gary Benson, relating the entire tale. A couple of days later we scouted the area that had been described, driving around all the back roads south of the main river, the Nottawasaga, until we found the train tracks. Sheldon Creek would be about a ten-minute hike up the tracks, we theorized, and struck out with visions of 10-pound brownies cavorting before our eyes.

We fished the creek for almost its entire length on both sides of the bridge, working the big pool thoroughly, but produced nothing but a slew of tiny rainbows. If it had not been for the obvious evidence of the attention given to the railway bridge hole by the three brothers—the forked sticks still stuck in the stream bank, the beer cans (unfortunately) strewn about and an abundance of cigar butts littered all over the place, plus a couple of very large brown trout heads that could clearly be seen in the bottom of the pool—I am certain that my friend Gary would have been convinced that I was putting him on.

We fished the otherwise inconspicuous-looking Sheldon Creek several more times, but never at night, and caught nothing but small bows. This only proves my long-held aspired-to theory that the fishing is more important than the catching. We almost always prefer to spend our valuable fishing hours on waters that are aesthetically pleasing and at least look like they contain fish. Also, our few nighttime stream-fishing excursions have never proven to be enjoyable for one reason or another, so they, too, are vastly curtailed.

> Q: *It is true that the Old Guy is into the aesthetics of angling. It may also be true that the Old Guy himself is responsible for O'Fishol, and the mind boggles here, thinking what might have gone into that can.*
>
> *I have often said that one of the reasons I enjoy angling is that fish live in some of the most beautiful places on the planet. I learned this from my Old Guy. Often the places he wanted to show me lay beyond No Trespassing signs, but he taught me that this didn't matter in any profound manner. Here's a little poem that I hope illustrates something of this:*

THIS ONE

*This one is about sneaking
alongside a white brick bungalow
past windows snapped open,
the gauzy curtain sucked into the
moist dawn,
past the couple sleeping
there like two felled trees softened
by moss
through the backyard
where a beer can lies tumbled,
drunk,*

over the green twist-tie fence
down the slope, shopping-carted,
condomed,
across a path made by wheels,
man's fiercest invention,
through thuggish weeds
finally stumbling upon
a creek
four feet wide.

That's what this one is about.

And Finally, Newts

My experiences in using live bait for brown trout have pretty well run the gamut from the lowly dew worm to the somewhat more exotic chameleons known as yellow spotted newts. These little reptiles are seldom seen in the open in broad daylight, more often being discovered scurrying out from beneath an overturned log or rock.

> Q: *Okay, here comes some more of that story about fishing on the Willowemoc River. I realize that in my capacity as editor/commentator I should have tried somehow to organize things structurally, to pull both halves together. But I think (this is my claim anyway) I wanted to give you some sense of how the Old Guy's stories come out, which is very rarely all at once. He begins a story and then something happens: he thinks of something else, he forgets where he is, a big brown trout darts out from underneath a log and takes a run at his lure. It could be minutes, hours, even days before he sticks a finger into the air and says, "Oh, yeah. Where was I . . . ?"*

On that brief second honeymoon to New York City some forty years ago, I found myself leafing through an outdoors magazine in the lobby of the hotel while waiting for my wife to escape the clutches of the beauty salon. An article about an area in the Catskills, only an hour or so north of the city, caught my eye with this title: "Fishing & Camping on the Willowemoc."

The story was written by a fellow who had camped beside this tributary of the world-famous Beaverkill River, and it described his fly-fishing efforts and results. I had never heard of the Willowemoc River, but like almost all trout anglers had certainly read many tales about the Beaverkill. Unbeknownst to my missus, I had secreted a tiny ultralight spinning outfit in the trunk of the car, although she had cajoled me into agreeing that our little holiday would not become "just another fishing trip!"

It proved to have been an auspicious choice, as I won a head-to-head confrontation with a big brownie who was disturbing our sleep by the pool. It eventually fell victim to an "artfully presented" live bait, a newt. The tale was described in the earlier chapter, but to complete the sequence of events, I should mention that two more nice browns fell to our approaches with spinners on the Willowemoc the next morning.

The three trout were cleaned and, after a little sweet talk at the local fish-and-chip store in the village, deep-fried in batter. The proprietor was quite willing, in exchange for the big brown, to prepare them for us, and we took them along with a substantial portion of fries with us on our trip back to Toronto. They made a great treat and lunch, dressed with a little lemon juice and salt, as we headed for home along the New York Throughway.

CHAPTER THREE

Fishing for Browns with Artificials

. . . .

I suppose it was Izaak Walton who first fished for brown trout with artificial lures. Venerated by thousands of trout fisherman as the patron saint of troutdom, old Izzie began fishing for browns with live bait, moved on to fur and feather and finally experimented with crudely made spinners, probably fashioned from his wife's jewellery.

Spinners, Wobblers and Plugs
. . . .

Although most anglers today seem to prefer fishing for brown trout with flies, this wonderful import to our shores from Europe can readily be enticed and captured on artificials—anything from spinners to wobblers and plugs. Probably more brownies are actually caught on spinners than on any other type of lure—or fly. I have probably irritated my fly-fishing brethren once again with that statement, but I would defend it on the water anywhere. If this were not true, there would be no need to declare many rivers or stretches of same off-limits to all but fly-fishers.

Although my buddies and I prefer fly-fishing to reap maximum pleasure in our brown trout pursuits, when conditions are suitable, if we are fishing for the pan and not simply indulging ourselves in the aesthetics of the long wands, we use ultralight spinning tackle. Most often, this means arming our reels with 6-pound test Magnathin monofilament, not to give us an edge in battling large fish, but to cut the loss of our spinning lures to the unavoidable snags where the browns are customarily located.

Silver, unadorned Vibrax or Mepps spinners are usually the lure of choice, and although they are more difficult to control in comparatively shallow waters, small wobblers will also take browns when fished carefully. Well-made spinners in the hands of an expert can be controlled in streams regardless of the speed of the current and their depth. Because they offer much more resistance to the water pressure when they are being retrieved than a wobbler possibly could, spinners are more efficient in streams and rivers than wobblers are. Wobblers are preferable in the still waters of lakes and reservoirs, since they can be fished in deeper conditions with greater ease than spinners can. In the first month of the season, casting-off points or rocky shoals in 5- to 15-foot depths will often find browns working the bottom in search of crawfish and stonefly nymphs.

Once the waters warm, Rapala and Flatfish plugs trolled slowly in the midrange of the thermocline at 56° to 58°F in lakes will also occasionally produce good brown trout fishing. Browns are normally located at slightly warmer levels of the thermocline than are brookies.

Using Spoons in Lakes

Plantings of brown trout in the Great Lakes have been extremely successful, since the abundant supply of smelts, alewives and other forage fish provide the wherewithal for sensational growth and startling catches. If you want really big brown trout for your wall, work the inshore waters of Lakes Huron, Erie and Ontario.

Unlike most bows, both browns and specks are fall spawners. Lake browns can be caught by trolling Crocodiles and similar spoons in 10- to 20-foot depths, preferably near river mouths. Breakwalls, harbours, boat docks and the like all provide potentially memorable results for the angler with enough patience to cast repetitively, hour after hour, until one of these behemoths wanders into the shallows from the depths, sees, then strikes the lure.

The spoon should be worked just off the bottom in these conditions, with an occasional touch or even rest on the bottom. A brownie seeing the lure stirring up a little sand or mud will often be more interested than it would otherwise. Definitely resist the temptation to simply toss the lure out and reel it in, as it seems most anglers are wont to do. Anglers who impart a variety of actions to their lures with rod-tip twitches and stop-and-start retrieves will entice more trout into striking than will anglers who simply depend on the inherent action of their lures.

Most record browns caught during the past ten years have been caught by inshore anglers fishing in this manner. The records have been growing from 20-some-pound fish to well over 30 pounds. Rick Matusiak has caught many browns in excess of 20 pounds while simply casting spoons off the Port Credit harbour walls.

Certain areas, notably artificial impoundments, such as reservoirs and artificial lakes, usually dammed for hydro developments, also lend themselves to substantially rapid growth in stocked brown trout. Anglers in these locations often prefer live bait, but spinning with artificials and even fly-fishing will occasionally produce action.

Nevertheless, although the potential for a wall-hanger is certainly greater in the big waters than in small streams, remember: *It has been proven many times that actual catching time when fishing is less than 5 per cent for even the most skilled anglers, so concentrate on enjoying the remaining 95 per cent to its maximum!*

Casting Spinners in Streams

Most of my fishing buddies and I devote all of our brown trout fishing hours to moving water, such as streams, rather than the still waters of the lakes. The streams and their environment provide much more interesting fishing for us than vast expanses of open water do—whether the trout are cooperating or not.

Considerably more skill is required in casting a spinner to the doorway of a piece of cover on a small stream than in simply winding up and tossing it out into the wild blue yonder of a lake. You also need to know how to work the lure correctly and to adjust the speed of your retrieve to the vagaries of the current if you want to catch browns and not spend most of your time extricating your spinner from snags below, on and above the water's surface.

Fishing your spinners with a manual pickup reel has a big edge over using one equipped with a full-bail pickup spinning reel. With the line on your fingertip, you can begin your retrieve at the exact moment the lure strikes the water. When you're fishing small waters, having this ability enables you to begin working the lure immediately, before it settles to the bottom, as would happen otherwise in shallow waters.

When stream fishing for browns, you should also keep in mind that the recalcitrant brownie will turn tail and disappear into its cover if you are within its forty-degree cone of vision. Therefore, you must place the lure as close as possible to the cover with the initial cast to avoid drawing the fish too far out into the pool, where it would see you and turn tail. Should the cast be made inaccurately so that the lure does fall short of the cover, the best course of action is to yank it out of the water immediately, taking care not to bury it in your eyes or ears.

All these challenges, dealt with correctly to the best of our ability most of the time, provide us with a level of satisfaction that cannot be achieved in any other manner of fishing for trout, especially brown trout. The only possible exception might be fishing during an evening hatch with dry flies we have tied ourselves.

Q: I would jump in here, eagerly, with an anecdote of my own, except that I haven't caught many brown trout. I do have a photograph sitting near my desk here, a picture of me holding one aloft, grinning broadly — I'm grinning broadly, the brownie is displeased — but I cannot recall the circumstances under which it was taken. I know that I was on the Ganaraska River; I know that I was fishing in the company of the Old Guy. The truth of the matter is, I have very few memories of specific fish. I have instead the very agreeable impression that part of my life has been spent ambling alongside a little river.

CHAPTER FOUR

Fly-Fishing for Browns

. . . .

Fly-fishermen, in general, consider the brownie their fish. Unfortunately, many of these folks disdain all other methods of fishing for trout, especially browns, and often have few qualms about displaying their contempt for spinning or live-bait anglers, regardless of their skills. I have on occasion been haughtily reproached for even suggesting that I often fish with spinners for browns. Fortunately, the true anglers in the fly-fishing fraternity realize that as pleasurable as it is, theirs is not necessarily the ultimate angling method.

Having in all probability irritated large numbers of fly-fishermen, I must state that I would rather fish for browns with fur and feather than with tin, any day, providing conditions were suitable for that venerable pastime. By suitable, I mean clear rather than roiled-up waters, a reasonable amount of open area to allow for fly-casting and not just dapping the surface, as well as enough pools where the cover in the stream will allow a fly to be fished properly.

Rods
. . . .

In the United States and Canada, many brown trout watersheds are far too overgrown to permit waving a fly line back and forth. My favourite trout stream, the Ganaraska River, is one of these. The Ganny, as it is fondly called by its aficionados, encompasses a large area only an hour's drive east of Toronto and comprises several branches and tributaries, all eventually merging into the main flow before emptying into Lake Ontario. There are resident browns in the Ganny that could tip the scales at 10 pounds and more, and these are not escapees from the polluted waters of the lake.

Although over 80 per cent of this river drains through forest and bush rather than meadowland, there still is enough fine water with sufficient room to wield a fly rod. Nevertheless, to be able more easily to negotiate the bush between the fishable stretches, we limit ourselves to rods not exceeding 7 feet in length. Our favourite is a little 6-foot split-bamboo, 5-weight wand that we build ourselves. Most of my fishing buddies have built the same rod, and in deference to the river we call it the Ganny.

If you are a rod builder or would like to have one of these lovely, fast-action rods built for you, here are its vital statistics.

Gord Deval's Light-Action Hollow Built and Fluted Bamboo Rods
. . . .

Measurements in 64ths of an inch at 6-inch intervals. Splines should be planed down to $3/32$ inch before fluting to $1/16$ inch. Taper fluting away from ferrules, leaving splines solid for $2\frac{1}{2}$ inches in both directions.

6-FOOT GANARASKA SPECIAL FLY ROD

Butt Section
Butt Ferrule

22	22	22	20	19	17	15

Tip Section
Ferrule Tip

15	14	10	9	7	6	5

> Q: *The Scarborough Fly and Bait Casting Association's members build rods throughout the winter, although I never did. I knew immediately it was the kind of intricate, painstaking labour at which I would suck royal. I do, however, own such a rod, built and presented to me by Gordon after the publication of my book* Fishing With My Old Guy. *Which you likely still haven't purchased. All right, I'll stop; I won't mention it again.*

Lines

. . . . .

There are many fly-fishermen who have adopted the principle that it is somehow more sporting and pleasant to use rods as long and light as possible while employing fly lines as light as 1 and 2 weights. Nevertheless, if you fish for the pleasure of the pastime, then equipment that will perform to your beck and call with minimum effort is essential. Specifically, that means not only terminal tackle that is balanced correctly but rod–line–leader combinations that contain at least a little power and speed.

I remember watching in awe while a number of "fly-fishermen," wading in New York State's famous Beaverkill River—and all dressed to the nines—would make as many as a dozen

false casts before releasing the line and presenting their fly—
all of 20 or 30 feet away! I am sure that the brown trout, with
which the stream is heavily stocked, must have experienced
vertigo with all those fly lines flailing interminably back and
forth over their heads.

Just for fun, the chap I was fishing with, Leon Schwartz, and
I took up a position a hundred feet or so downstream from the
last fellow we could see in the river, then, while standing on
shore (sans waders), proceeded to fish the pool next to him. It
was no problem for Leon and me to place our flies that far upstream using the double-haul technique and fast rods with
weight-forward lines.

The line we recommend for almost all stream fishing conditions is a WF5F (weight-forward number 5 floater). For those
anglers who may not know how these designations are
achieved and what they mean, the significant factor in fly line
size is the weight of the first 30 feet, less the foot or so of level
line at its very front end. Each individual numerical category
represents 30 grains. Therefore, a number-10-weight fly line
means that the first 30 feet of line weighs in at 300 (30 x 10)
grains, while the first 30 feet of a number-8-weight line would
weigh 240 grains. The first 30 feet of a 5-weight line would
weigh approximately 150 grains.

This classification system is based on the fact that it is the
first 30 feet of line beyond the rod tip that determines the load
on the fly rod when you are false-casting. The actual weight
will vary somewhat from one manufacturer to another, but all
seek to conform to the system to the best of their ability.

We use weight-forward lines rather than the more popular
double-tapers because they can be fired out with a minimum
of false-casting, provided the angler knows how to perform
the double-haul procedure. Less line motion in the air above

a feeding or resting brown means the quarry is less likely to be spooked.

Double-tapered fly lines do have their purpose, though. Having a longer front taper than a weight-forward line, they can provide a more delicate presentation when you are fishing dry flies on still water. Another advantage of the double-taper is that as the lines age and begin showing wear and tear, they can simply be stripped off the reel and reversed before being refitted.

Used in conjunction with the double-haul, however, the weight-forward fly line allows the caster to fire tight loops incredible distances with little effort, whereas a double-taper, with the heavier belly of the line still in the rod guides, slows down the rod action and decreases the likelihood of shooting the line without additional false casts. For a concise description of the mechanics of double-haul fly-casting, see pages 73 to 77 in Part 1.

Mastering the double-haul might seem a little mind-boggling after you read the instructions, but the exercise is certainly worth the effort. Anglers who study and practise the cast will reap the rewards of their patience.

Leaders
. . . .

Regardless of your fly-casting proficiency, without a properly balanced and correct-length leader, you will find it difficult to turn it over completely to accurately present the fly. Very few commercially manufactured leaders operate as efficiently as a hand-tied leader fashioned to the following formulae.

In competitive tournament casting it is imperative that the leader fully extend if the caster is to obtain all the distance, or precise accuracy, from his efforts. The fly-fisherman who also wishes to maximize results over the long haul will observe correct leader guidelines.

Here are sample leader specifications for various purposes, along with the criteria for successful leader performance.

Fly-Fishing and Casting Leader Specifications
. . . .

For best results, fasten sections together with four-turn barrel knots.

1. DRY FLY: Suitable for small streams and small flies. For larger flies, number 8 and up, increase tippet size to .010″. For flies smaller than number 12, decrease tippet size to .007″.

Butt—length and diameter of each section: 22″ .025″, 18″ .020″, 14″ .017″, 12″ .013″. Tippet length and diameter: 18″ .009″. Total length—84″ (7′).

2. TROUT FLY: For larger waters and those requiring a delicate presentation. For flies bigger than number 8, increase tippet size to .010″. For flies smaller than number 12, decrease tippet size to .007″.

Butt—length and diameter of each section: 22″ .025″, 20″ .020″, 18″ .017″, 16″ .013″, 14″ .011″, 18″ .008″. Total length—108″ (9′).

3. BASS BUG: Suitable for large streamers, bass bugs or other large flies that create excessive air resistance.

Butt—length and diameter of each section: 26″ .028″, 22″ .022″, 18″ .017″, 14″ .014″, 12″ .012″. Total length—92″ (7′8″).

4. LAKE FISHING LEADER: For casting nymphs, streamers and larger flies when more distance is required, such as when the canoe or boat should be kept as far away from target as possible.

Butt—length and diameter of each section: 32″ .026″, 27″ .023″, 24″ .017″, 22″ .013″, 19″ .011″, 20″ .008″. Total length—144″ (12′).

These specifications are guidelines only. The diameters can vary as much as .002" without greatly affecting the leader's overall performance, although the individual section lengths should be adhered to reasonably closely.

Generally speaking, for leaders, stiffer monofilament will perform better than the limp mono used for spinning. Limp mono can be used effectively for the tippet, though. The theory behind these leaders is a progressive reduction in the weight of each successive section (weight and length), allowing the smooth transfer of the energy created in the line and leader by the caster to flow right through to the tippet and the fly.

If there were too long a level section or tippet, or other uneven weight distribution, it would be difficult to achieve good, consistent fly-casting results. Also, unwanted knots are likely to develop in the leader, notably weakening its strength.

Leaders should always be lightly rubbed down before fly-casting with a piece of chamois or rubber to remove the memory placed in the monofilament from being stored on the fly reel. Care must be taken not to be overly exuberant in this exercise, though, as too much heat can weaken the leader. Leader kits can be purchased containing a dozen or so spools of properly identified (strength and diameter) monofilament to facilitate construction of your own leaders.

Here is a simple test to determine if your leader will perform adequately. Hold it at the butt end. If it is properly balanced and rubbed down, you should be able to turn it over (fully extended) using only your arm and a simple flick of the wrist. If the leader does not execute in this manner, you should either throw it away or try to correct it according to the above formulae.

Q: *Leaders, leaders, one of the banes of my existence.*
   One can purchase, you know, tapered leaders from the

*tackle shop, but the Old Guy disdains them. (I have them
secreted about my person and tie them on when he's looking away.) I do, however, also own one of the aforementioned leader kits and am sometimes inspired to get out
some leader specs and tie one up. I have to be in a very odd
mood, but it happens sometimes. The problem here is knots.
Gordon showed me years and years ago how to tie lines of
dissimilar diameter together—I guess it's called the Blood
Knot—but I have never really understood it and am too
ham-handed and fat-fingered to execute it. Occasionally I
pull one off, which gives me the impression (false) that I am
capable of it, so sometimes I try to tie up a leader.*

Flies
. . . . .

If one were able to accurately calculate how many fly patterns
have been devised to lure brown trout from their hiding places,
including those created by fly-tiers using their own imagination, I am certain the total would surpass the number of fly-
fishermen in Canada and the United States.

Every one of these flies would probably take trout—occasionally—in specific situations. One of the cardinal rules in
fishing, however, is that all the laws of averages are in the fish's
favour and therefore successful anglers are those who do
everything within their power to reduce those odds.

You cannot catch trout if your fly is not in the water. Most
fly-fishermen spend far too much time selecting and changing
flies, constantly poring over their fly books and going through
their fly boxes, hoping to find the magic solution for those days
when the trout seem to have lockjaw.

Most fly-fishermen carry an inordinate number of patterns.
Some would not dream of heading to the stream unless they

were equipped with hundreds of patterns in every conceivable size, colour and style. Anglers who merely adhere to the patterns that previously helped them create full creels have far greater success than do those who waste their valuable fishing time poring over their fly books and boxes.

With rare exceptions, I believe that carrying no more than a half-dozen flies in two or three sizes is all that is necessary to catch browns. I understand, though, that for many anglers, the pleasant hobby of tying their own creations, whether standard patterns or otherwise, is almost as fulfilling as fishing with the flies themselves. There definitely is a fascination in fooling a trout with the product of one's own artistry and workmanship.

Because the best choice of flies for browns greatly differs from one area to another, I am reluctant to recommend more than a few patterns. Following are my favourites for browns, several of which you may recognize as also being my preferred selection for brookies.

The Sutton Despair (see pages 83 to 86 in Part 1), either the peacock or seal-fur version, is tops as my choice in almost all situations, conditions and areas. Only the size would vary according to the size of the quarry and the clarity of the water. The clearer the water, the smaller the fly—and vice versa.

My second choice of flies for brown trout would be a sparsely tied Muddler Minnow. This pattern can be mistaken by the trout for either a grasshopper or one of their more common foods, the sculpin minnow. Muddlers work equally well fished on the surface with a twitching motion (grasshoppers), or among the bottom rocks and gravel with a darting motion (sculpins).

A third fly in my repertoire that occasionally gets a workout on brown trout waters is the very simple Deer Hair Caddis, with just a touch of green silk at the rear of the fly, simulating the larval worm peeking almost imperceptibly out of its case.

My buddy and I caught four browns just last week. We kept a couple for supper and when they were cleaned discovered that their stomach contents included crawfish, sculpins and a handful of caddis larvae. As I am writing this, though, it is still early May and their menu will certainly change as the fishing season progresses to include more insects and insect larvae.

When the various hatches of terrestrials, including mosquitoes, black flies, mayflies, stoneflies and so on, appear, a great deal of fun can be had as the browns leave the security of the depths and their cover to pick off these tasty morsels from the surface. Dry-fly-fishing comes into its own under these conditions, especially in the evening, when the insects prevail.

With a can of Muskol repellent in one pocket and a head net in the other in case the skeeters and black flies are really obnoxious, my fishing buddies and I will head for the stretches of the Ganaraska or Grand Rivers that are open, rather than those deep in the bush that we favour most of the time. Although this is a bit of a conundrum, if there is an evening breeze, the fishing is more comfortable when it isn't contained by the bush, while conversely the insect hatches are usually more prevalent in the open stretches as well.

Unless there is a predominant hatch of mayflies or stoneflies, my first choice in these conditions is almost always an Adams, usually in a fairly large pattern, size 8 or 10. I very seldom use any flies smaller than 14, as I have seen far too many trout badly hurt, even if I am using barbless hooks, when they engulf tiny flies in the 18 to 24 sizes. It is also much easier to remove a larger hook from a trout's jaw, where a bigger hook normally takes hold, than a minuscule one that is inhaled, as small ones often are. I know that once again I am contradicting traditional procedure as it is customarily accepted by most fly-fishermen, but in addition to being less injurious to trout, with few exceptions, larger flies will also attract larger trout, especially browns.

The Adams has withstood the test of time for thousands of anglers and is my choice for browns whenever mosquitoes are buzzing around, which seems to be—at least in most of the areas that I fish—almost always. Although the body of the original pattern is tied with grey seal fur, I will sometimes fashion the Adams's bodies from quill, either from a stripped grizzly hackle feather or a porcupine quill. The quill body seems to more closely resemble that of a mosquito than those tied from fur.

Tied with the hollow porky quills, they also float better than the fur-bodied Adams. They can be tied in the classic pattern with the hackle tip wings set upright, representing the live or emerging insect, but more often than not we fashion them in the spent position simulating the dead insect. It is a great deal easier to imitate a dead insect: no motion is required, and the fly looks very realistic. With the upright wing pattern, it is difficult to create natural-looking movement.

A great fly for brown trout on larger waters is the magnificent creation of one of the greatest fly-fishermen who ever waved the long rods, Lee Wulff. Although the expression "long rods" generally signifies fly rods, it is a matter of record that Wulff's preference was for smallish fly rods like our Ganny model, even when fishing for Atlantic salmon.

Lee Wulff was my hero in the outdoor writers' fraternity and one of only two or three of that brotherhood whose opinions on matters angling I never questioned. Although his hands were so large that he could have picked me up by the top of the head if he had wished, his ability as a fly-tier was redoubtable.

Although he was not the first fly-tier to use tufts of deer body hair for wings in his patterns, Lee took the use of this buoyant material (deer hair is hollow) to new heights with his flies, the White Wulff, the Grey Wulff and the incomparable Royal Wulff, my favourite.

From the time I was a youngster and was allowed to go downtown by streetcar by myself to attend one of his film and talk shows in Toronto, my respect for Lee Wulff as an author and a person never waned. But it reached new heights one day about ten years ago.

His wife, Joan, had invited me to participate in a fly-fishing festival in Roscoe, New York. At that time I held the North American record for Anglers' Fly Distance, and the Catskill Fly Fishing Club, which organized the festival, had decided to include several of the fly-casting disciplines as competitions in the fair. I was thrilled to be invited and to have the chance to promote our comparatively unknown sport of competitive casting and, even more important, to have the opportunity to possibly meet my lifelong angling hero.

I fully expected that I would be assisting and perhaps teaching some of the intricacies of accuracy and distance casting, but upon arrival I was told that the organizers expected me to just compete and do my best. They assured me that there were a few casters in the organization who would more than simply test my mettle.

It was disappointing to learn when we entered their beautiful museum and clubhouse that Lee might not be there, as he was off somewhere indulging in his other favourite pastime, flying his ancient airplane. Although Lee was eighty-two years old at the time, his age had hardly restricted him in any of his activities.

The first day of the festival and competition was extremely well attended. There were fly-tying booths, bamboo-rod builders, antique fly-fishing equipment and the like in one area and casting competitions in another. The last event scheduled, the Anglers' Fly Distance competition, was to be staged in a field near a pond where the accuracy course was laid out.

The club certainly had a few casters who could handle their equipment with expertise but were still not quite ready for the competitive trail. One of the greatest thrills of my life was about to occur, however. As Joan Wulff and her assistants were getting ready to conduct the distance game in the field, a tiny airplane came roaring out of nowhere, buzzing the field and competitors and seeming to fly perilously close to the ground.

"Hey, everybody," Joan shouted, "never mind him, it's just my old man. It's Lee . . . that's his way of letting us know that he's back. He'll probably show up here in a few minutes and want to cast the distance game with you guys after he puts that thing down somewhere."

I could hardly contain my enthusiasm, but I thought, he's eighty-two years old. It would be embarrassing for us . . . probably not Lee, though . . . if he were outdistanced too badly. What should I do?

I said to Joan, "If he wants to cast in the competition, what do you think . . . should I back off, or what?"

She seemed taken aback by the question and assured me that her husband was still very capable of throwing a long line and possibly even beating me at my own game.

While we were still discussing the question with a couple of other competitors, we saw an imposing figure striding forcefully toward us across the field. Lee Wulff had a dominating presence that was due to far more than just his being a big fellow, well over 6 feet tall and 200 pounds. His craggy, weathered appearance, simple, well-worn clothes and booming voice all added to the effect.

He came directly toward where I was standing, readying

my tackle. Without a trace of a smile, he announced loudly enough for everybody to hear, "Hey, Deval, Joan tells me that you're worried that I might be a little upset if you thrash me in this thing. Well we'll just have to see about that, won't we? 'Cause I'm gonna throw the game anyway, and I've got five bucks here that says I'm gonna kick your butt!"

It is almost impossible to put into words the feelings that raced through me, being addressed in this manner by the man whom I had been attempting to emulate for all those years—in a very small way, of course. Obviously I had to accept the challenge and wager, although the outcome, at least in my mind, was pre-ordained.

After all, I thought, the man is eighty-two years old. If I were to lose, I would either look foolish or be accused of not giving it my best shot. Still, if I win, will I simply be thought of as beating an old man?

In retrospect, these many years later, it is easy to see that I had no choice. My documented distances in the Anglers' Fly were a matter of record, and most of the men and women attending the event had been told what results to expect from our efforts. I had to cast to the best of my ability, whatever the consequences.

The luck of the draw had me throwing last, immediately after Lee Wulff. Most of the earlier competitors surprised me by tossing quite respectable casts of 100 to 120 feet. Then a hush fell over spectators and casters alike as Lee's name was announced as the next competitor.

As he strode toward me and the starting line, he suddenly turned and, before I could wish him good luck, bellowed, "Better give me *your* outfit, Deval. I think we should both use the same equipment so you can't say I whupped you because I had a more powerful rod or something. Okay?"

Like a bantam rooster beside him, I mustered up my courage and said as I handed him my equipment, "Good luck, Lee. But you're in over your head, you know. This is one bet I cannot lose."

Using my rod and line, equipment that was totally foreign to him, this senior citizen and hero to all trout fishermen proceeded to make mincemeat of the results recorded by the casters who preceded him, with a wonderful score in excess of 130 feet. I congratulated him when he finished his five-minute stint and said something foolish, like, "You sure made it tough for me, but get your five bucks ready anyhow."

Casting the Anglers' Fly Distance competitively requires the same attention to detail that is necessary in throwing a long line when fishing, except the double-haul has to be executed with tremendous hand speed, something that is entirely unnecessary when fishing. The timing for this takes a great deal of practice in order to throw a number 10 30-foot shooting-head fly line the incredible distances that the top tournament casters achieve.

My long cast that day was only about 150 feet but easily enough to win the wager and the tournament. I accepted Lee's congratulations, but when he begrudgingly peeled the five dollars off a roll of bills to pay off the bet, I said, "I'll accept it all right, but only if you let my buddy here take a picture of you handing me the fiver, okay?"

He agreed to the request, and that photo, the eighty-two-year-old Lee Wulff towering over me with a scowl on his face, his arm extended as he handed me the money, is one that I treasure. When someone poring over my many albums of fishing pictures asks about it, I gleefully say, "That's just Lee Wulff paying off a five-dollar fishing bet that we had!"

Remarkably, this icon of the trout-fishing world was able to cast farther than any of the much younger competitors there, with the exception of the only bona fide tournament caster in the event. On his birthday the following year, Lee was feted by the United States navy on the huge aircraft carrier *Magnificent*, with thousands of his admirers on hand to congratulate him.

Not too long after that honour, while flying his treasured plane, Lee Wulff was killed in an accident that many described as tragic. I am certain, however, that if Lee had been given the opportunity to choose how he would make his final exit, it would have been either while wearing his patched-up waders and fishing in a set of rapids in Labrador or Newfoundland or while buzzing about in his beloved Cessna.

Now when I fasten a Royal Wulff to my leader tippet, I do so with a certain reverence.

Q: *The reason Lee Wulff was able to do so well, of course, is that the double-haul is largely a matter of timing. Physical strength helps, but not so much as being able to feel the rhythm of the physics, the tension and the release. Add to that a certain belief that it's going to work . . .*

I remember receiving counsel from Allyn Ehrhardt, another of the competitors at the North American Casting Championships in Cincinnati. I was standing off to the side, patiently practising my double-haul. He watched me for a bit and then advised that it must be executed with "vigour and conviction."

Allyn's words have stuck with me. I still can't execute the double-haul all, or even most, of the time, but I try to do it—and everything else—with vigour and conviction.

One other dry fly that has produced browns for me several times when nothing else seemed to work was the Mashigami, a fly that begins as almost half a pound of deer body hair before substantial trimming produces this superb floater. Half a pound might be speaking a little facetiously, but the Mashigami, which is also a fine dry fly for big brookies, does look like it would make a fine old-fashioned shaving brush before its necessary pruning.

Some might consider this to be almost sacrilegious, but the Royal Wulff appears to be a somewhat refined version of the much older Mashigami, which originated in a trout-fishing camp in northern Ontario in the early 1920s. The fly is completely fashioned from natural uncoloured deer hair, with the body, tail, wings and hackle all heavily dressed.

I deliberately have not touched on the myriad fly patterns popular in both the east and the west, such as the Hendricksons and Cahills, for the simple reason that another whole book could easily be written just listing these, without delving into the many other factors required to become a good fly-fisherman. Many fine books, such as Ray Bergman's classic, *Trout*, contain descriptions of which flies are popular in which areas.

An Easy Gourmet Fish Recipe

Since most trout that I am lucky enough to catch are put back into the swim, I consider myself to be basically a catch-and-release practitioner. I do occasionally keep a trout or two for a dinner treat, however. My wife, Sheila, and I have eaten many scrumptious meals featuring trout cooked in a variety of ways, but I recently decided to try a method that is widely practised along the Costa del Sol on the Mediterranean coast of Spain.

We have been fortunate enough to vacation in that area several times and enjoy the way the local fish are prepared, both in the seaside restaurants and by fishermen cooking their catches right on the beach and selling them impaled on sharp sticks to passing rubberneckers like us. The fish grilled along-side the boardwalk, redolent of olive oil and garlic, are impossible to ignore.

These fish are not trout, but sardines—not the kind that we in North America are most familiar with, packed in cans, but fish 12 to 18 inches long, freshly caught just off the beach by fleets of small boats. On the beach, the vendors clean the fish and marinate them for a short time in a mixture of olive oil, lemon juice, coarse salt and crushed garlic. They gather drift-wood to make compact little fires, and the sardines, suspended on sharp sticks, are grilled alongside the hot coals, frequently basted with the oil-and-lemon-juice mixture.

I prepared an 18-inch brown trout in almost the same man-ner, using the same marinade. Since I didn't have a driftwood fire, I used the broiler in our oven. I slit the skin on the trout in several places on both sides and flipped the trout when the skin turned brown and crusty. Then it was broiled for a few more moments on the other side until it, too, browned. Absolutely delicious!

Rainbow Trout

The Pot o' Gold

· · · · · · · · ·

The pot o' gold is not at the end of the rainbow; it *is* the rainbow, the mighty rainbow trout!

Several factors have contributed to the tremendous growth in popularity of freshwater fishing in North America, Britain, New Zealand, Australia and even South Africa and South America in the last fifty years. The introduction and exportation of spinning equipment to the rest of the world from countries such as France and Switzerland meant that fishermen everywhere suddenly all felt like experts. Now they were able to cast without fear of backlashes, fish with smaller, more productive lures, cast farther than ever before and, most important in the majority of situations, catch more fish. Tackle manufacturers in almost every country jumped on the bandwagon, and with so much competition for the eager market, inexpensively priced spinning equipment became readily available.

The advent of closed-face spinning reels in America and Japan further increased the popularity of freshwater fishing. It now became a sport that anyone at any age could participate in with only a modicum of expertise yet still achieve results that they might only have dreamed of before.

About the same time that the spinning phenomenon was overtaking the angling world, rainbow trout stocking programs were emerging throughout Canada, the United States and many other countries. When the success of these undertakings became apparent, the stocking programs were soon accelerated virtually everywhere.

It was obvious to biologists that the rainbow trout, basically native to the northwest coast of North America—and in a number of inland lakes, where a slightly different member of the species, the Kamloops trout, also provided superior sport for anglers—was able to thrive and propagate in waters that were not necessarily suitable for other trout. Initial plantings were made in the upper Great Lakes in the thirties and forties, and the far-ranging bows rapidly worked their way through all the lakes in the chain.

These trout and their progeny retained the principal characteristics of the sea-run version, the steelhead trout, rather than those of the Kamloops trout of the inland lakes. That is, they would run the rivers in the spring searching for suitable gravel beds in order to perform their spawning rituals, then head back to "sea," spending the rest of the year in the cool depths of the upper thermocline, usually in the low to mid-fifties Fahrenheit.

In many areas there is a second run in early autumn in the same rivers. Whereas the rainbows' spring run up the rivers is for obvious purposes—the females scoop out redds (depressions) in the gravel where they deposit their eggs, followed by the often smaller male bows releasing their milt (semen) on the eggs—scientists are still debating why some of the fish also head for the rivers in the fall.

One possible answer to that conundrum seems rather obvious, at least in the lakes that have also been seeded with salmon. The salmon, unlike the bows, are fall spawners, and the enormous quantities of large roe deposited by these fish, also well upstream in the rivers, creates a powerful attraction for the bows frequenting the same waters.

As mentioned in Part Two, brown trout plantings and natural reproduction in the Great Lakes and its rivers have also increased considerably, and browns are fall spawners in the same rivers and tributaries as the salmon. As a result, there is a virtual smorgasbord of caviar for the bows to fatten up on to help sustain them through the long winter months they spend in the depths of the lakes.

Numerous plantings of rainbow trout have also been made in thousands of inland self-contained, spring-fed lakes where the fish are landlocked, with no rivers to run. Like brookies, however, bows have little success in producing progeny, though they go through the motions anyhow. There are only a few exceptions to that, and only in large inland waters, possibly those with upwelling springs on rocky or gravel shoals where the eggs would be able to germinate without becoming lost in layers of silt.

Rainbows are easy to to raise in hatcheries, however; in fact, the exercise is so productive that innumerable groups, such as fishing clubs and community groups, operate their own hatchery-like operations. These groups, with permission from provincial and state resources commissions, trap the spring-run fish, strip the eggs and then fertilize them on the spot with milt from the also entrapped males.

The fertilized eggs are then transferred into wooden nursery boxes placed in cold, spring-fed brooks until the resulting rainbow trout fry or fingerlings are large enough to release into the wild. These bows will eventually return to the same streams, where they will spawn. Because of all this propagation, natural and otherwise, there are now more rainbow trout available to more fishermen in more waters than all the other species of trout combined.

For example, in southern Ontario, virtually every trickle, brook, stream and river flowing into Georgian Bay and Lakes Huron, Erie and Ontario supports a run of rainbows in the spring, with most also providing action once again in the early autumn. The huge growth of the fishing tackle industry has kept pace with the rainbow fishery, and these two phenomena have developed a symbiotic relationship.

Hence the title of this chapter. The now ubiquitous rainbow trout has proven to be the pot o' gold for anglers everywhere, as well as for the fishing tackle industry.

Q: *We are discussing—if you will allow me to get scientifical on you—the anadromous rainbow trout. That word "anadromous," which I drop into many a conversation, not all of which have to do with fishing, means that the fish go up and down the rivers. On the West Coast, they go down the river into the ocean, where they become huge. This involves a process called "smolting"—the fish become "smolts"—which enables the trout to deal with salt water. (This whole subject of the anadromous rainbow trout involves some really keen terminology. For example, unlike salmon, steelheads don't die once they've spawned, at least not the first couple of times. They rest up for a bit and journey back to the ocean. During this resting period the fish are "mending," and once they've completed it, they are "mended kelts.") Here in Ontario, with the fresh water, the fish don't technically smolt, so I suppose rainbow trout don't become true steelheads. But they become large and beautiful and perhaps the greatest challenge/thrill an angler can have.*

The rest of Part 3 will examine rainbow trout fishing in a slightly different categorical fashion from fishing for brookies and browns, the reason being that the seasonal factor plays a much more important role in the bow fishery than in the others. Even the fish themselves, as we will see, are transformed, changing colour from one season to the next. Almost everything pertaining to successfully angling for rainbows is tied to the respective seasons, and for most anglers in most areas, the spring and fall steelhead runs take precedence.

CHAPTER TWO

The $\mathcal{S}$pring Steelhead Run

. . . .

lthough rainbow trout can be caught throughout the year in a great variety of locales, it is the spring steelhead run in the rivers that stirs the blood of huge numbers of otherwise rather placid fishermen.

The descriptive tag "steelhead" was originally applied to the bows on the North American west coast that escape the Pacific Ocean once or twice annually to swim up thousands of miles of glacier-fed streams and rivers. When the bows arrive in the streams, their flanks still glisten in their oceangoing coats, a gorgeous silvery or steel blue, topped with a metallic greenish hue. Many anglers also refer to the steelheads as steelies.

As the fish traverse the river to their respective spawning grounds, they gradually assume the trademark coloration from which they originally received the rainbow trout designation. The overall coloration soon becomes more of a predominantly greenish hue, with a slash of red from the caudal fin (tail) to the gill covers. As in almost all animal species, the males adopt far brighter colours than do the hens. In many waters the males are also highlighted, like spawning male brook trout, with elongated cream-coloured and black accents on their undersides. Whereas their river-running odyssey contributes to the metamorphosis of steelheads into rainbows (colour-wise), in many inland lakes and ponds where bows have been planted these lovely trout retain the high colours of the rainbow all year. One only has to observe the hatchery-raised rainbows clustered in a supermarket fish tank to see what I mean. All the bows will have the same coloration as a springtime stream-running rainbow.

The springtime steelhead trout run is referred to by thousands of anglers (and fishermen) as the opening. This is, in most areas, the opening of the trout season, at least in the rivers and in much of the brown and brook trout water as well. It is also the time when lines are checked for wear and tear; waders are checked for leaks; lures, hooks and split shot are replaced; and often exploratory sorties—without tackle, of course—are made to one's favourite steelhead flows to check out the status of the stream and its finny population. The best way to check waders and hip boots for leaks (not while being worn) is to place a light bulb on an extension cord down the legs, one at a time, in a dark room such as the bathroom, in the evening. Any leaks or wear spots that need patching are easily discovered in this manner.

Fishing with Live Bait
. . . .

Although more skilled fly-fishermen are working steelhead trout waters these days—and taking fish on their fur and feather presentations—most steelies hooked during this time of year fall prey to either spinners or bait fishermen.

Any live bait will take the spring-run bows on occasion, but worms, minnows and roe bags are the most common weapons of choice, with roe bags being the most popular bait for steelhead trout. Although crawfish and minnows provide bows with most of their natural sustenance during the rest of the year, the steelies, often seemingly more interested in sex than food, will nevertheless chomp down on dime-sized bags of nylon scarf containing trout or salmon eggs.

The bags can be fashioned from fresh roe or from preserved or frozen eggs obtained earlier. The most successful steelhead anglers seldom tie roe bags larger than a dime. Many induce the steelies to strike with bags containing only a single salmon egg from a chinook caught six months earlier and preserved either in a brine solution or in powdered borax.

Roe bags are best fished in a natural drift simulating eggs freshly deposited by the females. Although the spring-run steelheads appear to eat little, they will indulge themselves on wayward spawn that has drifted away from the redds. For this reason, many fishermen include a Styrofoam bead, or piece of foam, in the bags before tying them off. The extra buoyancy assists in keeping the bags from being caught on bottom while at the same time contributing to the natural appearance of the drifting bait.

Weight is required in order to cast the bags, as well as to control them in the current. The weights most commonly employed are split shot, placed a minimum of 18 inches up the line from the roe bag. This can be a single shot, the size depending on the current, or, as most bait fishermen seem to prefer, a number of smaller shot spread out at intervals of an inch or two, also, of course, totalling the required weight for control and a natural-looking drift.

An alternative to roe bags, which are messy to assemble, is similar-looking lures fashioned from tiny pieces of sponge that are no larger than actual roe bags. The sponge is shaped with a sharp pair of scissors; different densities of foam provide varying results. The colours should approximate those of the natural spawn, yellow to orange. The naturally buoyant foam is fished in the same way as the real thing that it imitates, drifting pieces of spawn or single eggs.

Using Spinning Tackle

. . . .

Spinning tackle has been the most common terminal tackle used by roe bag fishermen, but in the last few years many have adopted the so-called noodle-rods-and-float-reel method of drift fishing. With this equipment, the soft action and long rods (12 to as much as 16 feet) allow the fisherman to use line as light as 2-pound test. The soft, elongated noodle rod absorbs the shock of strikes and leaping fish; with a conventional outfit, the slipping clutch of the spinning reel performs the same function.

Many still prefer to use a spinning reel on these long rods, giving them even more flexibility in battling the big ones. The float reels enable these anglers to work with lines equipped with sensitive floats, strung-out small split shot to maintain the line reasonably straight in the current, and small wide-gap hooks with roe bags. Hook sizes range from 6 to 12. Worm fishermen often use the same setups, with a single dew worm hooked through the egg sac.

> Q: *The Old Guy is now going to tell you that he prefers to use his regular spinning rod—with which he is very successful—so I'm going to take a moment to rhapsodize about how pleasing it is to use the long rod. I have had more experience on the West Coast than Gordon has, and that is where this gear first gained popularity. I know how fine it can be standing up to your waist in the river, leisurely lobbing your roe bag (or facsimile thereof) upriver, allowing it to tumble down. Mind you, much of the fineness has to do with the*

*surroundings, the mountains and the Douglas-firs and the
bald eagles circling overhead, waiting to see if you get lucky.*

*So it is a very fine thing indeed, very relaxing and
contemplative—until a steelhead hits, that is. The reason I
fish, I have often averred, is that I love those moments of
connection, when you suddenly realize there is a life force at
the other end of the line. When you are fishing steelhead,
there is an augmentation of both the life force and the sud-
denness. Your hands tighten around the butt an instant
before your consciousness realizes there's been a strike. Line
starts to peel off as the fish drives away. You pump up and
pray, pump up and pray, and if you're lucky you might end
up with a steelhead. Even when you lose it, there are sometimes moments of rare privilege. A steelhead, ticked off by
the angler's nasty little prank, will often breach, shooing
straight out of the water, catching and throwing off sun-
light, landing back in the river with an insolent splash.*

Although this combination of long rod and free spinning
(revolving) reel allows the fisherman to work over a satisfac-
tory 20- to 30-foot drift with a minimum of effort, many of us
still prefer to fish for steelheads with exactly the same outfits
that we use for brookies and browns—that is, smaller, lightweight spinning rods, open-faced stationary-spool (spinning)
reels and 6- to 8-pound test monofilament line, when fishing
either with bait or with spinners.

My own preference is for a 5½-foot lightweight stick with a
manual pickup spinning reel. If drift fishing with bait, which I
seldom do anymore, I can have my bait in the water precisely
where I want it with every cast without ever taking my hands
off the reel. This means the bait spends more time in the water,
and thus, in the long haul, there are more fish on the line.

But adhering to my oft-repeated adage, "It's the fishing (95 per cent of your time) that counts, rather than the catching (5 per cent of your time, if you're lucky)," I fish almost exclusively for steelies nowadays with either Vibrax or Mepps spinners. On some days the roe baggers will clean my clock, leaving me feeling lucky if I take a single trout, but on others, the spinners will do more than hold their own in competition with the long rodders. The bows seem to strike the silver spinners out of annoyance or frustration, occasionally on the first cast, but more often than not only after the lure has been jiggled by their noses a dozen times or more.

Using Plugs

Another lure used by a handful of steelhead anglers is the trusty old Flatfish in sizes x.4 to T.4. The favoured colours are contrasting combinations, such as the skunk (black with a white stripe on top) or yellow or orange with a black stripe on the back.

These plugs, along with number 5 or 7 silver Rapalas, work most efficiently in somewhat slower waters than in many of the more turbulent flows where the spring run occurs. They should be fished very slowly, kept almost stationary, allowing the current to do most of the work of activating the lure's action. As little weight as possible should be used in these conditions—only enough to get the lure sufficiently deep in the water.

Flatfish and Rapala plugs are both very light lures. the Rapala is constructed of balsa; therefore when you are using a weight such as a split shot a foot or so up the line from the lure, casting can be a nuisance, as the weight often precedes the plug and the hooks foul the line in the process. Here is a tip that will help you avoid this mess: as the line flies off the reel during the cast, allow it to gently rub against your fingertip. Your finger should caress the line loops, supplying just enough resistance to keep the plug travelling out in front of the sinker and thereby avoiding snarls.

Another tip will assist you in playing these powerful trout or any other fish hooked in fast-water streams and rivers: Keep your rod tip low to the surface of the water at all times until you are ready to either release or land your catch. In this way the steelie will have the entire natural drag of the current on the line, working against it and tiring it out.

Netting Your Catch
. . . .

Many a potential dinner or even wall hanger is lost at the moment the landing net is thrust in the trout's direction. First, never attempt to land a fish with a net unless it is played to the point where it is on its side, fins moving gently. Second, never try to scoop up the fish tail-first with a net. If the trout is to be released, it is better to not use a net at all; simply remove the hook with a twist of a pair of forceps or needle-nose pliers.

If netting your catch is your desire, however, make sure the net's pouch is wet and preferably sunk, and then angle enough of the frame into the water to be able to lead the fish quietly over the frame headfirst. When the bulk of your catch is over the middle of the frame, simply raise the net only until the fish is nicely ensconced in the mesh, not necessarily right out of the water.

Absolutely avoid the temptation to yank the net and the trout high out of the water in your jubilation. Many a fine fish and landing net have been the victims of that manoeuvre. The mesh can be torn apart from the excessive strain and the fish lost as it falls back into the swim.

I have also seen a lot of lovely trout lost because the fisherman, in his excitement and haste to apply the coup de grâce, simply slapped away at the fleeing fish, using the net like a fly swatter, until he either broke the line or knocked the trout free from the lure. The rule is to *bring the fish to the net—not the net to the fish!*

> Q: *These are all very useful tips, but I'm going to chime in here with one of my own. It is perhaps my only useful tip. If you want to catch a truly magnificent fish, one that requires at least photographing and perhaps even mounting, it is imperative that you carry no net whatsoever. If you carry a net, you will catch only fingerlings and tiddlers.*

Once they are reasonably tired out, rainbow trout can be immobilized simply by grasping them around the narrow area of the body immediately in front of the tail, usually referred to as the wrist area of the fish. This practice is called tailing. Tailing an Atlantic salmon, which has a caudal area even narrower than a bow's, has been the accepted practice for years but has only recently become popular with steelhead trout fishermen. Wearing a cotton or wool glove facilitates the grab, giving you more friction in your grip than can be achieved barehanded.

Caution: Do not attempt this with brook or brown trout, as the caudal area on these fish is larger in relation to their tails than that of steelies and Atlantics. The trout would slide right through your grip.

Wearing Polaroid Glasses

Almost all successful steelhead anglers wear Polaroid glasses in order to see through the surface glare of the running water.

That is not necessarily just to be able to spot their quarry but to be better able to determine the depths and identify rocks and other structures where the fish lie.

> Q: *Steelhead angling gives one the opportunity to become every whit as well-kitted a nimrod as the fly-fisherman. Not only does one need Polaroid glasses, they need to be affixed by some sort of tether so that they may dangle on the chest. Also dangling on the chest, attached to the very expensive fishing vest, one needs nail clippers, hemostats (or whatever those surgical blood-clamp things are called, which steelheaders carry for hook removal or in case an artery gets opened) and a system of clasps and loops for in-stream rod holding, allowing the hands to go through all the little pockets for weights, swivels and terminal tackle, which is compartmentalized in plastic containers made by a company called Scientific Angling. Then, of course, there are the waders, rendered from a material that* NASA *discarded as being too expensive to deal with, and watertight boots with felt bottoms so that one may gingerly step across the stones. And a wading staff, because the felt bottoms are almost useless on those stones.*
>
> *I should warn you that there is a corollary addiction that goes along with the angling bug, which involves the acquisition of stuff. If you think you may be susceptible to this and your finances are iffy, get out now. If, however, it appeals to you and you have more money than you know what to do with, consider becoming a steelheader. If you are a multimillionaire, consider becoming a fly-fisherman who fishes for steelhead exclusively.*

When the hens are scooping out the redds with their tails, building a bed in the gravel in which to deposit their eggs, they can easily be seen with the Polaroids and should be left alone to continue their spawning ritual. There are always other, more receptive fish that have completed the function, and like us after sex, they are usually hungry. Well, they don't smoke, anyhow!

I do not know why, but unlike big-water brookies, which can often be found challenging the heavier current above waterfalls, steelheads spend little time holding immediately above falls such as those created by beaver dams and other structures. Perhaps they prefer the more highly oxygenated, bubbly fast water beneath the waterfalls, probably to recharge their batteries before attempting to ascend the obstruction and continue their travels upstream.

Preparing Smoked Trout and Gravadlax

Fresh-run steelhead trout prepared as gravadlax or lox (cold curing) is every bit as delectable as salmon done in the same manner. Although further preparation is unnecessary, additional curing of this delicious fare in a smoker is a worthwhile exercise.

Steelies between 5 and 10 pounds are ideal for these recipes, as the fish fresh from the deep water of the lakes have a firmer flesh than summertime trout (resident fish that for one reason or another stay in the river all year round) or those that have lingered in the river for a while after spawning. Trout properly cured by either drying or smoking can be kept sealed in airtight plastic bags for months. Chances are though, that the fillets will be devoured long before then.

Gravadlax—or, as it is sometimes called, gravlax—is a method of dry curing the trout using coarse pickling salt, a touch of sugar, fresh dill weed and the fish's natural juices. So far as is known, the procedure originated in Scandinavia, when, before freezing and refrigeration, salt by itself was used to cure fish. Lox is the name for salmon or trout cured in a brine solution and a big favourite of the deli crowd.

Smoking fresh fish imparts another pleasurably unique flavour to the fillets. This gourmet fare is prepared either with heat (hot smoking) or without heat (cold smoking). The differences in the end product are substantial and will be explained in the following recipes, from my book, *Free Food 'n Fun*.

> Q: *Okay, now here he goes. As I've mentioned, when Gordon starts talking about food, listen up. By the way, the book he mentioned,* Free Food 'n Fun, *is all about roving through the wild and eating it. Not all of it, of course, but certain delectable parts of it. When he first told me about this book, I said, "Oh, yeah. Kind of like Ewell Gibbons."* Most of us recall him as the author of Stalking the Wild Asparagus. *The Old Guy, however, merely furrowed his brow and asked, "Who?"*

Deval's Recipes for Gravadlax
(Cured Smoked Trout or Salmon)

. . . .

GRAVADLAX (ALSO CALLED GRAVLAX OR LOX)
Ideally, this preparation is for trout and salmon weighing between 4 and 8 pounds. For larger fish, adjust the curing time accordingly. Or split the fillets laterally to approximately ½ to ⅝ inch thick.

Split and fillet the fish, then remove the small lateral-line bones with needle-nose pliers or forceps. Leave the skin attached and do not scale the trout (the scales are insignificant). Cut each fillet in two.

On a large cookie tray lined with wax paper, sprinkle an even layer of coarse pickling salt (never iodized table salt).

Cover the salt layer liberally with fresh dill weed. Place the fillets, skin-side down, on the dill weed. Completely cover the fillets with another layer of dill on the flesh side.

Lightly sprinkle fillets with sugar and then top off with a second layer of the pickling salt. Cover the fillets with another sheet of wax paper. Additional layers of all the ingredients may be added, following the same procedures. The fish must be kept in a cool place (but not frozen) for the curing time.

Place a board large enough to cover the stacked fish on top of the wax paper covering the fillets. Then place several bricks or other weights of about 6 to 8 pounds on top of the board.

After about eighteen hours, drain the accumulated moisture before carefully turning the fillets over (flesh-side down). Replace the dill with fresh dill weed, top and bottom (note: no additional salt required), before replacing the board and weights. Cure for approximately another twelve hours.

Rinse the fillets thoroughly under a sprinkler and pat them dry with paper towels. Leave the drying fish out at room temperature on a wire rack, skin-side down, for an hour or two, or until a shine forms on the flesh side. The gravlax is ready to enjoy at this point and can be kept in the refrigerator for two to three months or frozen in airtight packaging for six months. To eat, slice thin pieces, always slicing in the direction of the tail, and place on buttered bagels, crackers or rye bread. Or add slivers of lox to scrambled eggs or salads. A thin, very sharp knife (new Rapala) or electric knife should be used for the slicing.

GORD'S SMOKED TROUT

Smoking is suitable for all trout and salmon, preferably fish over 20 inches, weighing more than 4 pounds. Smaller fish are better when prepared using a lox or gravadlax method. Leaner fish, such as whitefish, can also be used but require less time in the brine and more in the smoker.

This method of smoking fish is suitable for cold smoking, in which the hot plate (or other heat source) is separated from the fish and used only to produce smoke by heating the wood chips. The curing (cooking) is performed through a combination of the brine and smoke only—and does not result from heat. This method allows the fish to be eaten immediately, or if properly sealed and wrapped, to be refrigerated and enjoyed for several months.

The fish will remain edible and succulent if kept frozen for up to a year, provided that the fillets are wrapped in airtight packaging. I use zip-lock plastic bags and suck the air out with a straw before sealing them. That's as close as I can get to vacuum packaging at home.

Hot smoking of trout is simpler than the cold method, but the fish should not be kept for more than a week or two unless heavily smoked. Heavy smoking, however, tends to remove too much moisture, drying out the fillets. To hot-smoke trout, simply rub pickling salt into the fillets before placing them flesh-side down in the smoker.

If you use a very small compact smoker, the fish can be ready to eat in an hour or so. In the larger smokers, they'll be ready in about five to eight hours, depending on the size of the fillets. A slight cracking on the flesh side of the fillets indicates that they are ready.

Although cold smoking is my favourite method, it does require additional preparation. Fillets up to 22 inches are placed in a brine for eight hours, and fillets over 22 inches for up to twelve hours. I use a Coleman cooler for this purpose because it helps the brine retain an even temperature. The brine consists of the following ingredients and can be used several times if the fillets placed in it are clean and free from mucus. The amounts are approximate, and the recipe can be adjusted to individual preferences.

THE BRINE
1 gallon cold water
1 pint white vinegar
2 cups brown sugar
2 cups coarse pickling salt
½ cup pickling spices
3 or 4 garlic cloves, crushed
1 or 2 large onions, thinly sliced
½ cup chopped dill, preferably fresh,
    but dried may be substituted

Mix ingredients well with a wooden spoon. Place fillets in the brine, flesh-side down. Turn fillets every couple of hours, and keep the brine well stirred.

Remove fillets from the brine, lightly rinse or wipe, and pat dry with paper towels. Allow fillets to dry further until a shine develops on the flesh side.

(If you wish, the cured fish can be enjoyed *thinly sliced* at this point, as *lox*.)

Hang smaller fillets in the smoker for twelve hours and larger fillets for twenty-four hours. Hickory, apple and mesquite are the preferred woods to be used in the smoker, either as chips or coarse sawdust. For most applications you need eight to ten 9-inch pans heaped with wood chips to do the job. Hot smoking takes considerably less fuel, as the heated fillets absorb the aromatic smoke much more quickly.

Enjoy!

CHAPTER THREE

Summer Bows

. . . .

After the three-week-long assault on the steelhead rivers ends, about the same time that black flies and mosquitoes begin emerging, the great majority of the fellows that tramped up and down the streams chasing the big steelies begin looking for more prevalent game with fewer diversions. Most of the trout, many of them bearing visible scars from errant (and in some cases, not so errant) hooks, begin working their way back down the rivers to the relative safety and deep water of the lakes.

> Q: *What Gordon's getting at with that "not so errant" remark is that some fellows—scurrilous scofflaws—drag large hooks across the river in order to snag fish while some resort to using spears.*

A difference of only a few degrees caused by rising air temperatures or a period of warm rains is all that is necessary to drive all but a few of the spring-run steelhead out to the lakes, leaving the rivers to a small number of large resident bows, hundreds of yearlings and two-year-old trout that have not yet developed the urge to migrate. Any browns and brookies native to the river now become easier to locate as well.

These permanent dwellers of the stream have stayed deep in the cover and usually well upstream to avoid the rambunctious behaviour of the bigger steelies, just as the steelies themselves get pushed around by the mighty chinook salmon when they find themselves sharing the same waters in late summer and fall.

The small, 6- to 9-inch rainbow trout are not much of a challenge to an angler. They will strike with abandon at almost any lure or fly and can be found in virtually any type of flow in the stream—shallow, deep, fast or slow, in the open or in cover.

It is best to concentrate on brookies and browns during this period, since they are much more interesting and present a greater challenge to an honest angler than do the little bows. If you really want a few small bows for the pan, however, it is imperative that they be cleaned, streamside, placed in an airy creel and interspersed with a little watercress.

Small bows tend to deteriorate quickly, as the flesh, tender to begin with, softens more rapidly than that of brownies and brookies. After cleaning them, simply wipe the cavity and skin with a damp paper towel or cloth and *never place them in a plastic bag*. Washing them in the stream contributes too much moisture, hastening deterioration, and plastic bags prevent air circulation while also containing heat and preventing natural cooling.

These fish-cleaning and preparation guidelines are basically applicable to all fish, but trout, especially small rainbow trout, are the most susceptible to improper handling. Many a fine meal has been spoiled by ignorance of the facts spelled out for your information herein. Nevertheless, having possibly deterred the reader's enthusiasm for summer fishing for rainbows, let it be said that the pastime definitely has its rewards.

Fly-Fishing for Summer Bows in Streams

. . . .

Fly-fishing for these little guys really comes into its own in the warmer months, providing one's tackle is appropriately matched to the quarry. Terminal tackle, rods, reels and lines should be restricted to the 3- to 5-weight outfits and use double-taper, floating lines. Six- to 7½-foot-long leaders are all that is required, and tippets can be as light as 2-pound test.

All barbs on the flies should be flattened with a pair of needle-nose pliers, keeping only a slight bump on the hook to assist in retaining the hook in the fish's mouth should you relax for a moment when playing your catch. If the tension on the rod and line is not maintained, the resulting slack in the line creates a condition whereby the hook might simply drop out otherwise.

Almost any fly will take summer bows, but watching these smaller trout pick flies off the surface, then dance around in leap after leap, attempting to shake free the offensive thing in their jaw, is a special treat that fly-fishermen look forward to in the summer. I find heavily dressed Adams or similar dry flies, skittered across the surface riffles, to be deadly for summer bows. Nymphs, streamers and small, brightly coloured wet flies will also produce.

Occasionally a bonus is offered up to the summer stream fisherman in the form of a much larger holdover rainbow or brown trout. With the lighter tackle and fragile tippets, this serendipitous moment then becomes an especially exciting challenge that can certainly test the angler's mettle.

In many large western rivers, as well as some of the larger flows in the East, dead-drifting a Despair or Stonefly Nymph through the deep pools will bring some of the larger bows out for a look at your offering. To obtain a natural drift, the line should be frequently mended as it drifts downstream from the upstream cast. A simple raising of the rod tip, followed immediately by a short forward stroke, will impart a little momentary slack.

As in almost all situations, casts should be made upstream with a minimum of false casting so as not to spook trout lying in the open. To create an even more natural drift with your nymph, the cast should be mended before the fly alights on the water. This manoeuvre is performed with an almost imperceptible wagging of the rod tip during the final false cast and before the line is released from the left hand.

Another advantage of this exercise, called the Lazy S Cast, is that the S bend that forms as a result of the waggle can be applied to the line either at the front (leader end) or farther back in the belly, giving you the ability to precisely control where the mended portion of line alights on the surface. Therefore, if you wish the fly to remain momentarily in quieter water on the opposite side of the current across the stream from the main flow, you merely waggle the rod gently at the moment the line is released in order to place the S appropriately.

If the current is close to your position, however, then the waggle to the rod tip is applied at the last moment before the fly touches down. That places the S squarely in the closer current, allowing the fly to rest for a moment or two as the line straightens in the less turbulent water before it is whisked away by the current. Very little practice is required to perfect this technique, which can be an invaluable weapon in an angler's arsenal, enabling a fly-caster to fish water that might otherwise be inaccessible to the proper presentation of a trout fly.

Nonetheless, there is a downside to this upstream, dead-drift fly-fishing, as it is much more difficult to discern a hit on the fly with the line slack as it is being retrieved. Any sudden straightening of the line, regardless of how slight, should be assumed to be a bow taking the fly, and the rod tip should be raised sharply to set the hook.

Becoming popular with many fly-fishermen, a fairly recent innovation developed on Alberta's Bow River is the strike indicator, a minuscule section (no more than ⅛ inch) of coloured fly line that is slipped over the butt end of the leader. When a trout takes the fly, the twitch of the strike indicator can be seen much more readily than the line itself, therefore facilitating hookups.

Fishing Lakes for Summer Bows

Fishing in lakes for rainbow trout during the summer once again calls for a different set of tactics. The bows seldom wander from the cooler depths, spending most of their hours in the upper strata of the thermocline and avoiding the warm surface waters.

An inexpensive, specially designed thermometer that takes and maintains the reading until it is raised and the temperature read, while also indicating the depth where it was checked, is an invaluable tool in determining what depth to fish. Battery-powered thermometers and depth indicators are also readily available. These employ a remote sensor attached to a marked cable that is lowered to locate the parameters of the thermocline. In most smaller inland lakes, they may vary somewhat from one body of water to the next but should be located from depths of 8 to 12 feet below the surface down to 15 to 30 feet below for the bottom of the thermocline.

Since rainbows prefer temperatures from about 58° to 62°F, normally found in the upper regions of the thermocline, the summertime angler who takes advantage of this knowledge will place more trout on his stringer than will an angler taking a haphazard approach.

Trout in these circumstances can, of course, be caught with spinning tackle, light line and live bait. But working a jig or wobbler through the upper portions of the thermocline keeps you busier, preventing your falling asleep and falling out of the boat—something we actually witnessed one day while trolling near a buddy of mine who shall remain nameless. Don (oops) enjoyed nothing better than still-fishing with a worm or minnow on a warm summer day.

A hi-density fly line with a Despair or Muddler attached to a long, 13- to 17-foot leader can also be used to plumb the depths for summertime bows. In the days before hi-density fly lines became available, it was difficult to fish effectively with flies at depths of more than a few feet. Today you can buy hi-d fly lines that sink as fast as the old-fashioned copper wire trolling lines.

I remember one day when I was working a big yellow bucktail jig on a shoal in Mosque Lake hoping to find a lake trout or bow scrounging among the rocks for crayfish. The shoal was about 30 feet deep and was on the edge of the thermocline.

I had already managed to catch and release a couple of lakers in the 3- to 4-pound class when on successive casts I could plainly see a big rainbow follow the jig almost to the surface before swirling away, leaving a cloud of bubbles in its wake. Several casts later it made another pass at the jig, disdaining the lure at the last possible moment.

I decided to try another ploy in our little scrimmage in an attempt to bring matters to more than a sheer battle of will and wits. I cut the jig off, then cut a foot and a half off the end of the line and retied the short piece to the back of the jig's hook.

A quick audit of my fly boxes revealed only one Despair left in good working condition. The others had either a leg or wing missing, but had been kept anyhow, as a one-legged Despair is still a deadlier producer than most other trout flies. I quickly fastened the good Despair to the dropper tied onto the rear of the big jig.

If the bloody fish comes off the bottom again for another look at the jig dancing off the shoal and up toward the boat, I thought, maybe, just maybe, he'll spot the Despair tagging along behind and think it's a freebie there, simply for the taking.

This sinister deception worked exactly as imagined. That beautiful rainbow trout now resides resplendently on my dining room wall. As I recall, it chased the jig to within a few feet of the boat before smashing the Despair so viciously that it almost tore it and the dropper away from its host, the jig. But Lady Luck was on our side that day, and after a lively tussle the big bow was soon folded into the net. It wasn't fly-fishing—but it sure as hell was rewarding and fun!

There are many fellows who label themselves fly-fishermen and who seldom if ever actually cast a fly but do enjoy trolling with the long rods while presenting their flies to the trout in this manner. Because the flies can be kept at the required depths while being trolled, providing that depth has been predetermined, the fly-rod trollers can sometimes fish circles around even the most skilled casters. Feathered streamers, sparsely tied bucktails, Woolly Buggers and various leechlike patterns all work well when trolled.

Spinners, the number one lure for springtime steelhead fishing, are seldom as productive in lakes during the summer and never should be used when trolling unless you are prepared to discard your line at the end of your outing. Should you suffer a brain cramp and forget that rule, as I have done once or twice myself after an hour or so of casting, then switching to trolling to give my arm a rest, there is only one way to rescue the twisted line before tossing it into the scrapheap.

First remove the lure and manually feed out 15 or 20 feet of line into the water behind the moving boat. Then, taking care not to lose control of your rod and reel, speed the boat up, allowing the drag of the water to remove as much line from the spool as necessary to get to the end of the twisted portion. Trolling the line in this fashion with the rod tip close to the surface for a few minutes will remove any twist, making it softer at the same time. A word of caution: Make certain the drag is tightened, or the entire line could easily escape the reel when you blink.

Plugs such as Rapalas and Flatfish are excellent trolling lures for summertime bows. Although both these plugs come in a wide variety of types, sizes and finishes, with over fifty years of trolling under my belt, I have condensed the selection to the few that have proven to be the most productive.

We like Rapalas in the lighter, floating models in number 7 or 9 in the silver finish. I believe the lighter floating models, with a balsa wood core, have a superior latent sensitivity and therefore provide better action at much lower speeds than would otherwise be necessary. Additional action should be imparted to the lure with the rod tip, anyhow, even when trolling.

A further enhancement of the action in a Rapala plug can be obtained by fastening a split ring to the lure's nose. That allows the plug's lip to naturally find the point of most resistance, which, of course, also means maximum lure action. We fish the Rapala floating models with a number 4 or 5 (depending on depth) clincher sinker fastened 2 feet up the line from the plug.

Carefully pinch the tab on one end of the sinker down on the line. Then make several turns around the sinker before pinching down the other end. There is less chance that the line will break at the sinker using this tip than if you just crimp the sinker on tightly, which flattens and weakens the line.

Finally, grasping the sinker at its ends between the thumbs and forefingers of each hand, bend it into a crescent shape. In addition to getting your lure down to wherever you wish, the bent sinker will then serve as a keel, helping to prevent line twist should you troll too quickly.

Flatfish have always been remarkably productive trolling lures. Although the original lures designed and made by Charles Helin were constructed of wooden bodies, the newer versions made from plastic are among the most popular of plugs for all game fish. The peculiar design of this plug, with its offset hooks and long, sloping, flat front, creates maximum resistance to the water, so even with little forward motion at very slow speeds, the lure oscillates madly from side to side, creating excessive vibrations in the water that have proven to attract a trout's attention.

Unquestionably a poor lure to cast, the Flatfish, nevertheless, is one of the best trolling lures ever made. As you should do with all lures to determine the speed at which optimum action results, study its action alongside the boat before putting it into the swim. The same bent clincher sinker system described for fishing with Rapalas should be employed when fishing with Flatfish. For best results, it should be trolled as slowly as possible.

We prefer either combinations of yellow or orange and black or contrasting finishes of red and white when trolling with Flatfish. The sizes for summertime bows in lakes will range from x4s and 5s to the larger T4s and U20s. Some work more slowly than the others, but they are all fine producers of summer rainbows.

Trolling with wobblers such as the famous Delphin Krocodile, the Gord Deval Crocodile or Little Cleos in silver or gold is also very effective in many waters. A periodic sharp pumping of the rod tip will cause the properly balanced Crocodile to veer off course dramatically; the erratic action attracts bows who are convinced they are seeing crippled or dying minnows.

Always confirm that your wobblers are equipped with bronze French treble hooks with points at least as far apart as the spoon is wide to maximize the hooking potential of the lure. Discard and replace any that do not meet these requirements, and you will increase your chances of success immeasurably. The French treble hooks are well shaped and extremely sharp. Providing your line tests at least 6 pounds, when these hooks are snagged on the bottom they can usually be freed with a steady pull on the line.

Do not use the rod for this exercise, as the line may break where it contacts the tip-top. Instead, simply wrap the line around your fist several times so that it won't slip and cut your skin as you pull on the snag to free the lure. Almost always, French trebles will straighten enough to allow the entire lure to be extricated with little difficulty. It costs less to replace a hook than an entire lure.

One might believe, therefore, that a hooked trout could easily straighten the hook as well, but that is not so. When the hook is snagged on the bottom, the pressure is on the hook point. When a trout is hooked, however, there is no pressure on the hook point, providing it has penetrated and passed through the jaw or lip. The strain is on the bottom bend of the hook shank and not the point, which is more easily bent back.

Another fishing procedure has gained considerable acceptance among anglers fishing inland lakes in the summertime. Consisting of a combination of trolling, live bait and attractors, it is especially effective when the temperatures peak in July and August and the bows retreat somewhat deeper into the thermocline to seek lower temperatures.

The attractor is called a gang troll, a collection of different shapes and sizes of spinners on a length, or several lengths, of wire with a substantial keel at the upper end to prevent the whole apparatus from twisting the trolled line into a hopeless mess. These gang trolls, also called Christmas trees by some anglers, vary in length from 18 inches to as much as 48 inches.

The smaller trolls can be employed on spinning gear, whereas the big trolls necessitate the use of wire line and trolling with heavy-duty casting reels. The business end of the rig is usually equipped with a long-shank hook fastened to one end of a 12- to 18-inch length of 8-pound monofilament, with a swivel at the other end secured to the Christmas tree.

A minnow with the hook threaded through its mouth and out the gills, with the point pushed through from side to side an inch or so behind the gills, can work wonders on these rigs. A little experimenting will quickly demonstrate where, precisely, depending on the size of the minnow, to place the hook in order to obtain the most natural swimming action without the minnow simply spinning rapidly.

Full-size dew worms also work well on summer bows fished in this fashion. Thread as much of the worm on the long shank hook as possible, usually about half its length, leaving the remainder to wiggle freely while being trolled. Flies or wobblers are sometimes used in lieu of live bait on gang trolls but seem to be more effective when used on their own.

I discovered many years ago that using a fairly stout 5-foot-long casting rod and an old Pflueger Summit casting reel equipped with 500 feet of .012-inch Monel wire line I could plumb the depths of the thermocline with considerable accuracy. When the weather was so hot that we spent almost as much time swimming as we did fishing, with the use of this equipment we were often able to take summer bows that were difficult to locate and catch in any other manner.

I calculated the amount of wire line that would come off the spool during one full crossing of the level wind as the attractor was fed out. Since I knew that the gang troll would descend on about a four-to-one ratio at the speed we trolled the contraption, it became a simple matter to troll precisely where we wished in the thermocline.

With my reel, for example, each crossing of the level wind would yield 12 feet of wire line; therefore, if we wished to fish in the middle of the thermocline, about 20 feet beneath the surface, seven crossings (84 feet of wire) would be stripped and fed out behind the moving boat. Descending at the rate of four to one, the gang troll and bait would be placed right where we wished, about 20 feet below the surface.

The huge glistening blades of the Christmas tree throw off great flashes of light, but the vibrations created by these large metal spinners are, I believe, even more valuable in stirring otherwise lethargic trout into action. Various combinations and sizes of the trolls were put to the same tests that we have performed with all of our lures at one time or another; that is, we studied them in the water to determine the optimum speed with which they should be moved through the water to maximize their action.

When fished, all lures—and live bait, for that matter—create vibrations in the water that may entice fish into striking for one reason or another. Rainbow trout, like all fish, have a receptor organ (ear) that receives (hears) these vibrations and transmits them to the trout's brain, where they are interpreted as prey, as competitors for their food or as other adversaries.

This ear is easily distinguished as a lateral line running

midway up the sides of the trout's body from the gills to the tail. In most fish it also signifies the top of the rib cage, which is handy to know when filleting to avoid cutting through the bones into the stomach cavity.

Christmas trees, with as many as eight of these big flashing blades churning through the water, create more noise and vibrations than any other lure or flasher that we have ever tested. When you are snorkelling and one is trolled near you, it sounds like a train with cracked wheels passing through the water. The fish come out to see what all the fuss is about, see the tiny morsel (seemingly swimming along behind all by itself), try to steal it from the troll and are hooked.

A little research is necessary ahead of time to determine the rate of descent of your lure and choice of trolling speed. You just have to experiment trolling your rig over predetermined depths, such as shoals with known distances to the bottom. Should it be necessary, the electric thermometer-depth gauge device described earlier does this job efficiently. If you are fortunate enough to have an electric fish finder, then the depth, too, is visible on the screen.

Even though the summer bows hang deep in the warm weather, there is the occasional evening when they desert the cool depths to feed on an evening hatch of mayflies or other insects. That is your signal to pack up the wire line rig, break out the long rods and fish the surface, or near surface, with floating lines, long leaders with either your "match the hatch" attempts or your favourite personally tied dry flies.

Lightweight spinning tackle with no heavier than 4-pound test line and number 1 or 2 silver spinners can also produce some exciting moments in these conditions. I have had splendid results on several of these occasions with trout rising all around me, although it soon became apparent that my customary modus operandi, working the spinner slowly and erratically, required immediate modification.

The trout were taking mayflies from just beneath the surface as they wiggled along trying to shed their larval skins and emerge as adults on top, where they would unfold and dry their wings before taking off to continue the cycle and mating dance. It appeared that the spinners had to be kept just beneath the surface and cranked in rapidly to somewhat simulate the nymphs or at least interest the bows in striking. Using these tactics produced surprising action more than once in the heat of summer when all else failed.

Those folks equipped with large boats suitable for braving the big waters of the Great Lakes can capture bows—and big bows, at that—all summer long with their electric downrigger equipment, depth finders, thermometers, global positioning devices and ship-to-shore communications. The downriggers merely allow fishermen to get and keep their lures at the desired depth while using comparatively light tackle. The light line is attached by means of a quick-release device to a cable with an enormous weight holding it at the intended depth.

The professional charter boat fleets and their captains on the Great Lakes also have the equipment and experience to guide and assist even the most ill-equipped but eager fishermen to a successful summertime rainbow trout excursion, providing they are willing to pay fairly big dollars for the service. Of course, they may also have to contend with huge brown trout and monstrous chinook salmon during the same outings.

Using the services of a charter operator, even the most inexperienced angler can catch bows on the Great Lakes in the summer. Given my druthers, however, I would rather fish the smaller inland lakes, not with a professional guide, but with a fishing buddy. Working streams, also with a buddy, with each of us taking our best shots in alternating pools, would be even preferable to that.

> Q: *Man, was that a lot of information. And the Old Guy didn't mention—I suppose because he doesn't do it—the belly boat. This is a fine way of getting about those little lakes in summertime. A belly boat is basically a glorified inner tube. It has a little seating arrangement and a kind of backrest. One sits in this contraption out in the middle of the water, casting with abandon in all directions. One casts in all directions because it's impossible to keep a belly boat aimed in one selected direction, but that's all right. Once the fly is cast, it sinks to the thermocline (or wherever serendipity dictates); one then kicks and propels the belly boat backward, dragging the fly gently along. One of the reasons I enjoy belly boating so much is that I imagine that the fish themselves are surprised to encounter me. As I take the hook out of their lips, I can almost read the thought in their eyes: "What are you doing way out here?"*

Rainbow trout, steelhead trout, bows, steelies—whatever you wish to call them, all easily the least enigmatic members of the char, salmon and trout families—provide great satisfaction, superb entertainment and fair-to-middling dining for anglers, while creating financial rewards for everybody associated with the fishing tackle industry. Therefore, it is not just a case of the pot o' gold being found at the end of the rainbow. The bows *are* the pot o' gold.

CHAPTER FOUR

Ice Fishing for Bows

· · · · · · · · ·

$\mathcal{F}$ly-fishermen will be pleased to know that they need not pack away their paraphernalia in the winter just because the lakes are covered with ice. Provided that they trek into their favourite inland rainbow trout lakes before the mantle of ice exceeds 2 or 3 inches of hard, blue ice with no snow on top, they can fish with their best and bushiest dry flies and have a remote—albeit improbable—chance of catching a trout or two. When the ice is barely safe enough to walk on and transparent enough to see through, one must assume that a rainbow trout searching for a feed can also see through the ice, right through to its surface.

Because the trout can probably see you as well as your fly, make a cast from as far away as you can with your bushiest, most colourful creation. If you are too close, the trout might be spooked and the entire exercise undertaken for naught. Keeping in mind where you have taken bows previously, drop the fly on the ice right above the area where you think one might be lying.

You must also be certain to select a lake that has one or more rivers feeding it where rainbows can spawn and thus become steelheads. Whereas ordinary, everyday bows would never be able to break through the ice to snatch your offering, a mighty steelhead might be able to accomplish this seemingly impossible feat. After all, they are not called steelhead trout for nothing!

Although the chances that this procedure would work are rather minimal, trying it could provide you with another tale to add to your library of fish stories, as well as a little off-season fly-casting practice.

> Q: *The Old Guy certainly has his mischievous side, but I don't think he's having us on here. He believes this can be done, probably because he's done it.*
>
> *But I for one have no objection to packing away my paraphernalia when winter claims the world. I stow my stuff away as willingly as a bear yawns and goes to bed. I content myself with thumbing through old magazines, watching television shows and dreaming about the springtime.*
>
> *For those who enjoy ice fishing, however, here's some information from the Old Guy.*

For the hardy angler who does not object to the trials and tribulations of hiking or Ski-Dooing through deep snow to reach his favourite rainbow trout lake, ice fishing definitely has its rewards. It can be a fine, cold-weather, physical fitness regimen, certainly superior to sitting on the couch, beer in hand, watching fishing shows on television.

Because they do not quickly deteriorate as they do in hot weather, bows taken in the winter retain their firm freshness and occasionally freeze before you get them home. If they are still frozen at the conclusion of your trip, they can be kept whole in their frozen state for at least a couple of months if properly wrapped in airtight fashion before being placed in your home freezer.

If they are thawed before reaching home, however, they, like most fish, should not be refrozen if you want them to retain their succulence, although they would still be perfectly good to eat. Larger specimens, over 5 or 6 pounds, lend themselves perfectly to cutting into 1-inch-thick steaks. A whole frozen fish can simply be sawed into steaks using either a hand or a power saw, the frozen entrails pushed out, and then the steaks can be wrapped two or three to a package.

Since few lakes retain a thermocline in winter, the water temperatures won't vary a great deal from top to bottom. The exception is shallow shoals, which may absorb a little heat from the winter sun and pass it on to the immediate surroundings. Springs, which have a consistently higher temperature than the lake itself, will also produce hot spots where the bows, searching for a feed, sometimes congregate.

Short of drilling holes and exploring with a thermometer, one easy way to often locate where springs enter the lake is to look for beaver houses along the shoreline. If possible, beaver will always build their abodes near springs. The water should be slightly warmer there, resulting in thinner ice, which in turn makes it easier for the beaver to build its exit and entrance holes above the latticework surrounding its home.

Fish 15 feet or so away from the visible part of the beaver's residence. If you set up too closely and manage to hook a bow, your chances of landing it are minimal, as the fish will likely dive through, under and between the many branches comprising the outer, underwater framework of the beaver lodge.

If you are familiar with the lake and its various depths and shoals, it is a simple matter to set up on the shoals and jig with a flashing spoon or Rapala ice-fishing jig. Fish these right on the bottom, as bows working the shoal for a feed are primarily searching for crawfish, sculpin minnows or the odd chub or sucker foolish enough to distance itself from the relative safety of the school it left behind in deeper water.

Although the wintertime bows can be caught on artificials, it stands to reason that live bait—worms, minnows or crawfish, specifically—will take far more fish than will plastic and metal contraptions that, generally speaking, are difficult to work in a manner that produces a lifelike action when you are fishing through a hole in the ice. The lure that comes closest to achieving that trait is the Rapala Jigging Minnow, which is designed to swim in concentric circles if fished correctly.

You must remove any plastic or paint from the hook points on this lure, though, as it could hinder the hook-set on a strike from a rainbow. Another tip when fishing these jigs is to tie in a small black swivel 18 inches above the lure. Otherwise, because of its continuous one-way circling, the line would develop uncontrollable twisting. Resist the temptation to overwork the lure; it will produce superior results if fished with only a gentle manipulation of the rod tip.

Then there are the mind-boggling ice-fishing preferences of that good buddy of mine, Rick Matusiak. Rick, perhaps the best rainbow trout angler I know, likes nothing better than to get out on the inshore waters of Georgian Bay, which is part of Lake Huron, when they first freeze over. A couple of inches of hard water is all that it takes to get him going.

But what really gets Rick's blood boiling and adrenaline flowing is the period when the ice begins to break up, as the wind and waves coming off the main lake cause the ice to heave and split into masses of grinding floes. I suppose it is the challenge and not just the fishing that excites him, but he takes this dangerous pastime to the limit.

He cautiously works his way out from shore, jumping from one floe to another, either backpacking or sometimes dragging a sled filled with his equipment, until he reaches his destination over the desired depth of water. Once there, amazingly, Rick sometimes catches as many as fifty steelhead trout in a single day.

This indomitable rainbow trout angler has even devised a system of underwater photography, with a monitor on the surface so that he can scrutinize the action on the bottom. The resulting videos are so original and well done that his photography has developed into a lesser, secondary career for him, and he now obtains filming assignments from a popular television fishing show.

But I would never suggest that Rick Matusiak's innovative ice-fishing methods be adopted, or even attempted, by anyone else.

> Q: *Rick's enthusiasm is monumental. He carries a little collapsible metal shovel with him at all times, which helps with clearing slush out of his fishing holes but can also be used as a paddle should he happen to find himself adrift on a piece of ice. Matusiak pushes things to the extreme, certainly, but his ardour is common here in southern Ontario. A few years back a huge piece of ice "calved" (I believe that's the term), carrying something like fifty anglers out into the middle of Georgian Bay. Rescue helicopters were sent, but many fishermen declined to be rescued.*

Few anglers are aware that there is another fishing treat in store for them that has become available in a number of areas, such as Haliburton County and the Land O' Lakes District in eastern Ontario. Normally applicable in lakes that are basically a put-and-take proposition, the legal fishing season has been extended in these and other regions to the entire year, with no seasonal exclusions whatsoever.

With winterlike conditions on some days and, at times, quite lovely weather on others, the period after all the leaves have abandoned the trees, cottages have been closed down and fishing tackle put away can provide yet another exciting spot of angling action for those wishing to brave the cold. Providing the rainbow lakes still do not sport a mantle of ice, it is not ice fishing, but for some reason that I have never been able to understand, fishing from a boat at this time of year seems to be twice as cold as a day spent ice fishing. When the opportunity arises to avail myself of this late fall fishing for inland lake rainbows and I am able to cajole a buddy into joining me, our cold-weather Ski-Dooing and ice-fishing clothing and footwear are trotted out and put to good use.

From our little car-top boat we work the shoreline, with either fly-fishing tackle or spinning gear, hunting for bows foraging the shoreline to fatten up before the long hard-water months. This is the one time of year that I don't automatically begin fishing with a Despair when using fly gear; I prefer to use bucktail or Polar Bear Streamer Flies in bright colours instead. I believe that nymphs, not being prevalent just before freeze-up, at least in the lakes that we can access in our area, are not something the bows are specifically seeking.

Minnows, also diligently working the shoreline for their own dinners, comprise the bulk of the fodder the trout are searching for before the freeze-up. One of the more successful patterns for bows at this time of the year is a quite simply tied Polar Bear Streamer on a long-shank number 2 tinsel-covered hook.

The body is fashioned with medium, flat silver tinsel, ribbed with medium, oval gold tinsel, and the wing is sparsely tied from natural polar bear. No tail, neck or throat hackle is necessary. The multifacets of the ribbed tinsel body create reflecting flashes of light in all directions, attracting the bows' attention, while the Polar Bear wing, being somewhat translucent when wet, provides a natural, minnowlike appearance. This streamer should be fished with spasmodic, darting movements right in the shoreline cover.

Spinning can also do an effective job at this time of year, with small silver wobblers or spinners worked in a manner similar to that described for cold-weather fly-fishing. One nuisance in the pre-freezin' season, whether you are fishing with fly or spinning gear, occurs when the temperature dips below freezing. Water coming off the spinning or fly lines onto the rod guides will quickly become ice, completely closing them.

Rather than attempting to chip off the ice, merely lower the rod into the water, wait for a moment or two to allow the water temperature, higher than the air temperature, to partially melt the ice and then swish it back and forth underwater several times. The guides will clear automatically. On extremely cold days, you may have to perform this manoeuvre every other cast.

On these very late fall outings, if you happen to be fishing with an aluminum boat and the temperature should drop below freezing, you must exercise extreme caution, especially if there is wave action on the lake; even a gentle chop could be the death of you. Case in point: A few years ago, a buddy, Bill Orpin, and I were enjoying a sunny but bitterly cold day of rainbow trout fishing in mid-December on a small lake in Haliburton.

It had turned out to be one of those rare days when the trout were striking so well that our flies were being torn to shreds by the hungry bows. Our attention was, of course, focussed entirely on the fishing. Foolishly, with our concentration else-where, we were completely unaware of the danger that was sur-rounding us.

Not until the small waves that had been splashing against the sides of our boat began to find their way over the sides did we realize the seriousness of the situation. Although we kept bailing out the water, much of it remained on the boat bottom as slush.

Finally, and probably moments before we sank, we were able to appreciate the enormity of what was occurring. The por-tion of the boat's freezing cold aluminum hull above the water-line had taken on a deadly coat of external ice, sinking the en-tire boat to the point where the waves were easily breaking over the sides.

Managing to keep down the ensuing panic that threatened to envelop us, we paddled ever so cautiously to shore. If we had started up the motor, we would have sunk on the spot as the rear end of the boat lowered and a deluge of water poured over the ice-covered transom. Luckily, we eased the now extremely heavy prow up against the shore, scrambled out and, catching our first breaths in a while, counted our blessings.

Using chunks of gathered driftwood (we did not wish to jeopardize our paddles) we banged away on the hull until most of the ice was freed before we clambered aboard and paddled cautiously back to the access landing where our car and car heater awaited us. I suppose many folks reading the previous paragraphs would probably think, and rightly so, that we must have been crazy to place ourselves in a position where our lives were in jeopardy simply to catch a few fish.

I remember many moments when I would to agree with that prognosis, such as when I look at the video of Rick Matusiak's favourite ice-fishing methods, leaping from one drifting ice floe to another to jig for early-running steelies, or during my struggles fishing for brookies in almost impenetrable bushes and cedar swamps while contending with raspberry canes, stinging nettles, poison ivy, quicksand, unseen logs and pits, everything obscured or disguised by 6-foot-tall fiddlehead ferns—and, often, all for a few 10-inch brookies, browns and bows.

But it is precisely these angling aberrations that take one beyond run-of-the-mill fishing, giving the sport a completely different element—and that, I believe, is what fishing is all about. It is the fishing that we enjoy, not just the catching!

As I have said many times, less than 5 per cent of even an expert angler's fishing time is actually catching time, so why not enjoy the other 95 per cent to the limit?

Q: If Gordon thinks it's cold and unnecessarily risky, I don't want any part of it.

I guess we've come to the end. What do you think of my Old Guy? He's quite a character, wouldn't you say? But I think you know by now that he knows how to fish, and he loves fishing, and he loves the world for giving him an opportunity to do so.

I shall leave him alone, now, to wrap up things as he sees fit.

I hope to see you guys out on the water.

$\mathcal{E}$pilogue

. . . .

$\mathcal{P}$eople often ask me why I only fish for trout. "You got something against bass and pickerel?"* they'll say.

"Hell no! I've got nothing against bass," I'll answer. "I've even got a couple of them mounted and on the wall in my rec room . . . mind you, they were caught almost sixty years ago.

"And as for pickerel, there's very little that can top a feed of pickerel fillets. I buy them whenever I see them on sale, somewhere or another. I used to fish for pickerel years ago, but I don't really think they're much fun to fish for."

The next question is usually, "What about pike?"

My response to that one sometimes raises hackles. "Well, they do grow big, don't they? But jeez, do they smell! They're bonier than hell, too, you know. Not only that, they're stupid. Did I ever tell you about the pike on the Broadback?"

How these fish (great northern pike) got the adjective great tacked onto their name is beyond me. I suppose it's because of the size that the toothy things reach in some areas. For example,

*Also called walleye in some quarters, in deference to our American friends, who have a small grass pike in the Northeast that they also call pickerel.

during the dozen or so trips my buddies and I have made into northern Quebec searching for a world-record brook trout, one of the most irritating obstacles that we have had to contend with were pike weighing as much as 38 pounds. Many of our flies and lures have been surrendered to these fish, even the smallest of which (often referred to by the derogatory term hammerhandles) possess a mouthful of extremely sharp teeth. Since we do not use any form of wire leaders when fishing for brookies, a fly or lure engulfed by a pike's yawning maw is automatically snipped off by its teeth, often without any sensation of a strike.

Those hooked on the lip or outside of the mouth have to be played patiently until they roll on their sides, when they can be brought in and the hook carefully removed with forceps. Sometimes a half-hour or more of valuable trout-fishing time is wasted; a pike has little suspense, excitement or trickery in its arsenal and so it is only its size and strength with which we must contend. Often, realizing that we are losing so much time, we will deliberately break off the line, even though that means forfeiting the lure.

Our disdain for these fish was further accentuated by a couple of rather bizarre incidents involving pike that occurred on the Broadback River. Most fishermen have heard that pike can be caught on just about anything with a hook attached; bottle caps, can opener, a fifty-cent coin or whatever. The stories are legion on this fact.

On one trip to this fabulous river in northern Quebec, old buddy and professional fisherman Pete Pokulok, casting just to the side of our little camp, hooked and brought in a pike that would have tipped the scales at about 15 pounds. He removed his lure and released the fish.

On the very next cast, however, the same pike struck again,

was brought in and, once again, released. This fish must have been attacked by an osprey when it was much smaller because it bore a quite noticeable scar on its back, probably from the bird's claws.

The second time it was released, seemingly not much worse for the wear and tear, it stayed right where Pete had placed it. Tired of the nonsense, he quit fishing, strode back and reported the incident with the foolish pike. "It's probably still sitting there if any of you guys want to have a go at it," he said.

With breakfast about to be served, nobody accepted the offer, but over the next few days, Pete's pike, now being referred to by all of us as the camp pike, was successfully hooked, landed and released three or four more times by one or another of us, simply to see if it would continue its cooperation. When fishing became dull, as it does occasionally, even on the Broadback, we could always nip over to the camp pike and produce a little fun and games.

Somebody suggested that we attempt to prove or disprove the myth that pike can even be caught on a bottle opener. It is true! We wired a hook to the can opener, tossed it out in our camp pike's direction and watched as it lumbered over and snatched the "lure."

Another Broadback River trip produced two more pike incidents worth mentioning that illustrate the reason for our contempt for this fish.

I was fishing upriver a few miles from camp with Gary Benson, he on one side of a beautiful pool below a set of small rapids and I on the other, when Gary bellowed across the river, "Fish on!"

Then, scornfully, "Sheeeit! I think it's a pike."

A moment later I also had a strike, and while he continued to play his catch, I also shouted, "Fish on!"

Then foolishly, I announced, "This one's a trout, Gare, I think . . . and a big one, too!"

He yelled, "Mine's going over your way. Should I break it off so it won't get in the way of your trout, or what?"

Precisely at the moment of his polite offer, his pike rolled on the surface 15 feet in front of me. Simultaneously my line, firmly affixed to my "trout," popped up out of the water, as did Gary's in exactly the same manner, but in the opposite direction.

"You're caught on my line, Gary," I yelled. "Let it go slack."

Suddenly, with egg all over my face, I realized what had occurred. "Oh no!" I moaned. "We've got the same bloody fish!"

As it was now on my side of the river, I brought the pike in and, unbelievably, removed both Gary's spinner and my wobbler from the inside of its mouth. The pike had struck at his lure and while he was playing it also struck at mine!

A day or two later four of us began fishing in and around another large pool below another set of rapids, when I reeled in my very first cast, minus my favourite Crocodile Wobbler. It had obviously been snipped off by a pike. I subsequently donated another lure to what I thought was another pike. Gary, opposite me and wading in the river, hooked yet another one, which he played for a few minutes before deliberately breaking it off.

My old fishing buddy Tony Whittingham, standing on a rock just downstream from us, then donated another couple of lures to what we suspected was a pool full of big pike. That totalled five lures in rather short order. The other fellows, deciding to move upstream to fish the next pool, then paused to watch me play and finally land one of the pesky pike that had been harassing us and stealing our tackle.

Holding up the 4-pound hammerhandle, I yelled above the roar of the rapids, "Come here and see this . . . and bring your cameras . . . you won't believe this one, guys!"

Keeping the pike in the shallows at my feet until they all arrived, I then hoisted the fish and, using my forceps, one by one, removed six lures from both the inside and outside of its mouth and distributed them to their rightful owners.

So much for pike!

In brooks and streams trickling through bush, meadows and cedar swamps, or on spring-filled inland lakes, fishing for brookies, browns and bows has an aestheticism that the warmer, weed-filled waters containing pickerel, bass, muskies and pike cannot duplicate. In almost every trout stream or lake where my buddies and I fish, we do not hesitate to cup our hands, when we are thirsty, and scoop up a drink of sweet, clean and cold, chemical free, water.

Watercress, found in and alongside virtually every spring-fed stream capable of supporting trout, assures us that the water is pure and safe to drink. However, I suppose with all the present-day discussion of "beaver fever" or, giardiasis, some precautions should be observed. One of my buddies carries a plastic, filter-type bottle in his fishing vest. Some others take water with them from home in cooler flasks. Anyway, from May to September, we seldom go home empty-handed, even if skunked in the fishing department, as there is always a supply of the delicious cress, which can be made into soups, salads or garnishments for just about everything.

Although I have caught literally thousands of brook, brown and rainbow trout over more than sixty years of fishing, it never ceases to amaze me how beautiful and varied the colours and markings are on these fish, even on the tiniest of brookies and browns. Compare these with the dull greys, browns and greens on the flanks and backs of pickerel, pike and bass. No contest!

Nor can tossing a line equipped with a float, hook and worm over the side of an anchored boat for bass, trolling back and forth on a lake for pickerel or fishing weed beds for pike or muskies compare with the challenges involved in fly-fishing or spinning for brookies, browns and bows.

Six hours of standing up to your waist in ice-cold fast water while fishing for bows in the spring steelhead run, with nothing between you and the frigid water but your waders and long underwear, is not necessarily a great challenge. Nevertheless, weathering the painful leg cramps that sometimes result afterward, occasionally in the middle of the night, certainly are.

Similarly, finding yourself mired in quicksand-like muck that is threatening to swallow you whole on the side of a minuscule brook in the middle of a cedar swamp and having to yell to your upstream buddy for help also presents an interesting challenge to the dedicated trout-fishing angler.

Another great challenge is to acquire the necessary expertise to become a successful cold-water trout angler. That is in a considerable contrast to the minimum competence one needs to catch warm-water fish.

In summation, although all fishing is balm for the soul, angling for brookies, browns and bows offers so much more to the angler that by the time I was a teenager, I knew that fishing for these trout was destined to be my lot in the world of freshwater sport fishing. It is one that I have never regretted.

Glossary of *Fishing* Terms & Gordisms

· · · · · · · · ·

Anadromous Migrating from the sea to spawn in rivers.

Angler A fisher-person who has accumulated advanced skill and superior knowledge and experience. According to my definition of the term, such a person is an angler rather than merely a fisherman.

Artificials Fishing lures that are not live bait.

Backlash A tangled line that results when the revolving spool of a bait-casting reel turns too fast for the speed and weight of the lure to keep up with it, therefore overrunning itself and tangling.

Bait-casting outfit A rod that is shorter than a spinning rod, 5½ to 6½ feet long, with a revolving spool reel. Customarily used when heavier equipment is required, as when one is fishing in heavy cover or for large fish, as well as when casting with heavy lures, necessitating the use of heavier lines.

Barbless hook A hook with no barb or one that has been flattened by the angler. A barbless hook can usually be removed from a trout's mouth without undue damage to the fish.

Boondocks Countryside, well away form city centres.

Bows Rainbow trout.

Brookies Brook trout, also called speckled trout, specks, squaretails, Quebec reds.

Brown Hackle The simplest of wet flies, merely a body fashioned from wrapped peacock herl with a soft, dark-brown neck hackle.

Browns Brown trout.

Caddis fly One of the many insect families of the order Trichoptera; it forms much of a trout's diet.

Caddis case The "house" that the caddis larva builds and carts around in the water. The case is constructed of materials easily located in the area, such as bits of grass, wood, sand and gravel.

Caudal area A fish's tail area. In trout, occasionally referred to as the wrist.

Chub A minnow common to most lakes and rivers.

Clincher sinker A lead weight, ½ to 3 inches long, split lengthwise with tabs on each end that can be folded over (thus, clincher) to anchor the line, which has been placed along the split weight. If the line is wrapped once or twice around the sinker body before the tabs are crimped, you won't have to apply undue force on them. If clincher sinkers are used to get the line deeper when trolling, the soft lead should be bent into a semicircle. That simple trick will allow the sinker to also act as a keel to prevent the line from being unduly twisted.

Closed-face spin-cast reel A spinning reel with housing surrounding the spool and a centre hole where the line emerges. Depressing a pushbutton with the thumb causes the line to be trapped against the lip of the spool. This reel is simple to use but has many drawbacks.

Cover Shelter where trout, especially brook and brown trout, prefer to spend most of their time. It can consist of rock piles, weed beds, trees, branches, logjams or even junk carelessly discarded by humans, such as tires and other car parts.

Despair A nymph created by Jack Sutton.

Dorsal fin The main fin on the backs of most fish.

Double-haul A method of fly-casting that enables the angler to cast farther and more efficiently.

Dry fly A trout fly tied to simulate an insect, either alive or dead, fished on the water's surface.

False-casting The back-and-forth movement of the fly rod and line as one extends line to the point where the fly should either be shot forward using the double-haul or simply placed on the water's surface.

Fingerling The stage in a trout's development in which it takes on some of the characteristics of the parent fish and begins to fend for itself.

Flatfish A lure (plug) that produces maximum wobbling action in the water because of its large, flat frontal surface, which provides great resistance to the water when retrieved.

Float reel A fairly large single-action reel, resembling a fly reel, used mainly by rainbow trout fishermen with their "noodle rods." Most are controlled by hand pressure on the rim of the spool.

Fluted and hollow-built rod A split bamboo rod of superior action and speed, which result from its construction. Each of the six strips comprising the sections of the rod is planed down before they are glued together, then each is also fluted with more material removed by fluting, or planing lengthwise with a special curved chisel-like tool.

Forty-degree cone of vision An area in which a trout can see in, below and above the surface, approximating a forty-degree inverted triangle above its head.

French hooks Fine-wire treble hooks made in France.

Full-bail pickup A wire encircling the spool housing of a spinning reel that can be flipped open to free the line for the cast but that snaps shut, engaging the line for the retrieve, when the handle is turned.

Gang troll An array of spinners from 12 inches to as much as 4 feet long; occasionally called a Christmas tree because of its ornamental appearance. A metal keel is included to keep it from devastating the line with all that spinner action. It is essentially an attractor with a short length of monofilament attached to a swivel on its bottom and with a lure, fly, minnow or worm as the actual bait.

Ganny A nickname for the Ganaraska River, a superb trout stream, an hour's drive east of Toronto.

Gravadlax A Scandinavian method of preparing trout or salmon using dill, salt and pressure. Also known as gravlax or lox.

Gregory, Myron A Californian who, along with Marvin Hedge, developed the principles of weight-forward fly-line construction and double-haul fly-casting.

Grizzly hackle feathers A black-and-white barred feather from the neck of a Plymouth Rock (occasionally called barred rock) chicken; used in many patterns for neck hackles or wings.

Hackle A feather tied in one or more revolutions around the collar of a fly so that the fibres radiate 360 degrees.

Haliburton A county about a three-hour drive north of Toronto that contains myriad lakes, many of which are splendid trout fisheries.

Herl An individual strip of feather radiating from the spline of an ostrich or emu tail feather.

High-density fly line A fly line constructed from material of a higher specific gravity than that of a regular floating fly line. These are available in different densities, depending on how deep you want to fish the fly. Being of a higher specific gravity also means these fly lines are smaller in diameter. Therefore, they create less air resistance and cast farther than the fatter, floating lines.

Ice fishing Fishing through a hole cut in the ice.

Ice-out A short period of excellent fishing in spring when a lake sheds its blanket of winter ice.

Jigging Fishing a lure or jig with a vertical motion of the rod.

Leader A connection between the fishing line and the lure or fly, most often a short length of wire when used for spinning and normally a considerably longer section of microfilament for fly-fishing.

Leader tippet A short length of light monofilament attached to the terminal end of a fly-casting leader. You can easily replace it without having to rebuild the leader itself.

Leather fly book A leather, pocket-size container for holding trout flies. It usually contains several parchment envelopes and metal clips or a small plastic or aluminum compartmented box.

Lox See *Gravadlax*.

Manual pickup A spinning reel without the full-bail pickup. The line is completely managed with the index finger, which takes the place of the full bail and gives the angler superior control of the line and the lure, both in the cast and in the retrieve in the water.

Matching the hatch Attempting to duplicate with artificial flies whatever insect is prevalent. The hatch refers to the adult specimens as they leave their larval stages and emerge on the surface of the water.

Mayfly Any of an order of terrestrial winged insects. Mayflies are one of the principal foods of all trout.

McGinty A black-and-yellow wet fly simulating a wasp or bee.

Muddler A trout fly designed by Don Gapen to represent sculpin minnows, a principal trout food located on the rocky bottoms of streams and lakes. The Muddler consists of bucktail over a wild turkey wing feather tied in streamer fashion. It also has a shaped large head fashioned from clipped deer body hair.

Muskol The finest insect repellent available. The active ingredient, as much as 100 per cent, is N-diethyl-tolumide, commonly referred to as Deet. Care must be taken, however, not to get it on your tackle or to use too much on your skin. It is quite effective simply used on your clothes near openings to bare skin.

Newt A 3- to 4-inch-long lizardlike creature, similar to a salamander.

Noodle rod A long, sensitive rod, used by rainbow trout fishermen. The long rods act as shock absorbers, allowing the use of very light lines when drift-fishing with worms or roe bags.

Nymph (1) One of the larval stages of insects. A principal food for all trout. *(2)* A trout fly fashioned to resemble the larval stage of an insect, normally fished on or near the bottom of a lake or stream.

O'Fishol A lure scent formerly marketed by the author. Although it may sound like nonsense, O'Fishol is based on ancient formulae used by both aboriginal Canadians and Portuguese fishermen. It serves a twofold purpose: to attract fish and to mask smells repugnant to fish, such as those of cigarettes, gas and oil, mosquito repellent and human beings. (Fish have an extremely keen sense of smell.)

Pickerel The enduring name for this succulent member of the perch family, often called walleye, in deference to anglers from the United States, where a small member of the pike family, grass pike, is also called pickerel. In almost all Canadian fish markets, this fish is still called pickerel—not walleye.

Planting A substantial introduction of fish to an area.

Plug A plastic or wood fishing lure, often shaped and coloured like small fish and designed to wiggle from side to side, simulating a fish's natural swimming action.

Polaroid glasses Glasses that allow an angler to see beneath the surface of the water regardless of the glare on top. A simple check to determine if glasses are truly Polaroid is to take two pairs and place an eyepiece from one against an eyepiece from the other. If both glasses are Polaroid, rotating the lenses will completely black out vision at one spot in the rotation.

Redd A depression, usually in gravel or similar material, where a spawning female trout deposits her eggs to await fertilization by the male. Redds are often constructed by the female, using furious twists of her tail and body on the selected spot.

Roe Fish eggs (spawn).

Seeding A light introduction of fish to an area.

Set lines Unattended baited lines.

Shiners Any of several varieties of minnows.

Slipping clutch An adjustable feature on spinning reels that allows the line to slip (by permitting the spool to turn) without breaking when unduly strained and without the angler's removing his hand from the handle. The clutch should be adjusted just below the breaking strain of the line—with a test applied accordingly to check the setting. The test should be made by pulling on the line extending beyond the tip of the rod and not by merely pulling it off the reel. The difference is considerable.

Smolt A young sea-run fish at the stage when it becomes covered with silvery scales and migrates from fresh water to the sea.

Snap swivel A combination fastener and swivel, which, if it must be employed to prevent line from twisting or to serve as a connector, should be kept to the smallest size that is practical for the weight of the lure, preferably in a black finish.

Spinners A fishing lure fashioned with a blade that revolves around a wire shank.

Split-cane fly rod A fly-fishing rod built from six sections (splines) of bamboo, split from the raw material. Each piece is planed into the selected taper before all the sections are glued together and fashioned into two- or three-piece finished rods. These can be constructed in a wide variety of patterns, depending on their intended use.

Split shot A round piece of lead that is split three-quarters of the way through and crimped on the line to get it down quickly. Split shot comes in a wide variety of sizes.

Sponge Tiny pieces of yellow or orange sponge fashioned to resemble fish spawn.

Stationary spool reel Another term for a spinning reel, differentiating it from revolving-spool bait-casting reels.

Steelhead The variety of trout that migrates to the sea or lake.

Stonefly Any of an order of insects with wings laid longitudinally along their backs. Another staple of a trout's diet.

Streamer A fly tied to represent a minnow. Most often fashioned with a feathered wing, but many patterns are tied with hair wings such as polar bear or bucktail.

Strike indicator A colourful, highly visible marker, either paint or minuscule heat-shrunk plastic tubing, fastened to a fly line tip. Its sudden movement is an announcement that a fish has struck or taken the fly.

Tailing Landing a fish by grabbing it near its tail.

Terminal tackle Rod, reel and line.

Terrestrial A winged airborne insect, such as a mayfly.

Thermocline A layer of cooler stratified water beneath the warm surface water in lakes. In smaller lakes the thermocline is normally located at depths of 8 to 15 feet below the surface and may be as much as 20 or 30 feet beneath the surface. Most trout prefer to inhabit the thermocline.

Throwing tin Casting artificial lures with a spinning rod.

Topographical maps Maps that are produced by government agencies and display a great deal of information useful to anglers, such as creek sources, back roads, cedar swamps, forests, trout ponds, altitudes and so on.

Tournament caster One who casts plugs or flies competitively for accuracy or distance or both. There are generally twelve recognized disciplines, three fly and three plug accuracies, and three fly and three plug distance games.

Treble A hook with three barbs.

Trout fishery A stream, river or lake area with conditions suitable for the maintenance of a healthy stock of trout and with reasonable accessibility for the angler.

Trout fry The initial stage in a trout's development after it leaves the egg.

Wand waver A fly-fisherman.

Watercress A delightful salad green growing along the edges of and in the water of many spring-fed trout streams. It has a unique, slightly nippy flavour and can be used in a wide variety of ways.

Well-kitted nimrod An angling neophyte who is dressed to kill.

Wet fly A trout fly designed to represent a dormant or dead insect, usually fished well beneath or just beneath the surface. Wet flies are also occasionally tied simply as an attractor and not to represent anything in particular except the fly-tier's fancy.

Wobbler A fishing lure, usually made of metal and consisting of a curved blade that moves from side to side when pulled through the water. Also called a spoon.

Wulff, Lee Perhaps the greatest fly-fisherman of all time.

Index

. . . . .

A/B Lake, 55–56, 110–12
Albany watershed, 25
Algonquin Park, 64
Allen, Don, 89–90, 96
Atwood, Carl, 14–15, 81

Bails, 4, 10, 61–62, 150
Bait
  chubs, 108
  crawfish, 44–45, 125, 126
  crickets, 44
  frogs, 44–45, 137
  grasshoppers, 44, 52, 125,
    137, 160
  grubs, 50–51, 52, 136–37
  lures and, 61, 108, 114–15, 139,
    200–201
  maggots, 50–51, 52, 138
  mayflies, 48–50
  mice, 127–28, 132–33
  minnows, 28, 43–44, 108, 125,
    178, 201
  newts, 45, 47–48, 145, 146
  roadkill, 51
  roe bags, 178–80, 182
  salamanders, 45
  salmon eggs, 179
  shiners, 108
  trout eggs, 179
  winter care, 109, 209

  worms, 28, 32, 34–35, 38–43,
    108, 125, 128–29, 139–44, 178,
    180, 201
Bass, 26, 61, 72, 97, 215, 219
"Beaver fever," 219
Beaverkill River, 45, 146, 154
Beaver River, 141
Benson, Gary, 121, 129, 130–31, 143,
  217–18
Bergman, Ray, 168
Blue Lake, 90, 91
Bow River, 195
Bows. See Rainbow trout
Brech, Jurgen, 95
Broadback River, 64, 68, 83, 96, 215,
  216–19
Brook trout
  bait, 38–52
  coloration, 18, 31, 219
  diet, 26–27, 42, 43–44, 98
  fly-fishing, 69–102
  habitat, 18, 24–25, 27, 28, 29,
    31–32
  ice fishing, 105–16
  jigging, 41, 113–15
  lures, 28, 35–36, 53–68
  size, 18, 35–36, 83
  spawning, 25
Brown trout
  bait, 47–48, 122–46

coloration, 19, 219
cooking, 121, 168–69
diet, 119, 122–23, 124, 148–49, 160, 161
fly-fishing, 148, 152–63
German, 70, 118
habitat, 18–19, 118–19, 148, 149
lures, 120, 147–51
size, 19, 119–20, 127, 134, 140
spawning, 149
temperament, 120, 124, 131, 151
trolling, 119, 148, 149
Brulé Lake, 96–97
Burns, Robert, 133

Caledon Club, 25
Cannon, Roger, 56, 68
Casting
    bait, 79
    competitive, 73, 77, 79, 163–67
    double-haul, 73–77, 155–56, 167
    false, 75–76, 93, 155
    fly, 72–73
    Lazy S, 194
    Pendulum, 10–11
    spiderweb, 79
    spin, 60–61, 72, 150–51
Catch-and-release fishing, 120–21
Catskill Fly Fishing Club, 163
Cavan Creek, 125–26
Char, 24. *See also* Brook trout
Christmas trees. *See* Gang trolls
Cleaning and preparing fish, 192, 203, 208
Clemow, Ray, 33–36
Compleat Angler, The, 39, 129
Cook, Dr., 16
Cooking trout, 16, 121, 168–69, 208

Credit River, 119, 126–28

"Dapping," 48–49, 152
Deval, Randy, 112, 134, 135
Deval, Sheila, 168
Deval, Wendy, 106–7
Dogs, fishing with, 108–12
Downriggers, 119, 204
Drift fishing, 180, 181, 193–94
Duncan, Ron, 126, 127

Ehrhardt, Allyn, 167
Electric equipment, 203, 204
Eppinger, Lou, 66

Fish-O-Buzz, 107–8
Flies
    Adams, 83, 98–99, 161, 162, 193
    Black Ghost, 94
    Brown Hackle, 80
    Brulé, 83, 96, 97
    Bucktail, 197
    Caddis, 160
    Cahill, 168
    Ches-croch-'n-ed streamer, 90–91
    Despairs, 1, 83–84, 85, 86, 87, 96, 135–36, 193, 196–97, 211
        Green, 83, 85, 160
        Peacock, 83, 84–85, 160
    dry, 70, 98–101
    Grey Wulff, 163
    Henrickson, 168
    Mashigami, 99, 100, 167–68
    McGinty, 90, 101, 102
    McStarkovitch, 96
    Mickey Finn, 94, 97
    Muddler Minnow, 39, 83, 94, 96, 160, 196

Muscarovitch, 83, 96
nymphs, 70, 89–92, 193
Parmachene Belle, 94
Royal Coachman, 94, 97, 99
Royal Wulff, 99, 100, 163, 168
Shaggies, 90–91
Stonefly Nymph, 193
Streamers, 70, 92–98, 211–12
weighted, 97
wet, 70
White Wulff, 163
Woolly Buggers, 197
Floats, 41, 180
Fly-fishing
brook trout, 69–102
brown trout, 152–68
rainbow trout, 193–95, 196–97,
203–4, 206–7, 211–12

Ganaraska River, 6, 40, 97, 124, 129,
132, 134–35, 151, 153, 161
Gang trolls, 28, 201, 202, 203
Gapen, Dan, 100
Gapen, Don, 83, 94, 100
Georgian Bay, 110, 141, 175,
209, 210
German brown trout, 70, 118
Giardiasis, 219
Gibbons, Ewell, 187
Glen Major Club, 25
God's River, 25
Grand River, 161
Grass pike, 215, 220
Gravadlax (gravlax), preparing,
186, 187–88
Great Lakes, 119, 149, 153, 173,
174, 175, 204, 209
Gregory, Myron, 15

Haliburton area, 55–56, 64, 104,
210–11, 212
Hatch. See Matching the hatch
Hatcheries, 20, 174, 178
Helin, Charles, 199
Hemostats, 185
Hip boots, 178
Hooks
barbless, 88
sizes, 44, 51, 88, 93, 101, 108,
161, 180
Sproat, 87
treble (French), 54, 59, 65, 200
wooden, 53

Ice fishing, 20, 103–16, 206–14
Ice on boats, 212–13
Ice-out fishing, 26–27, 96–97

Jigging, 196, 208–9

Kamloops trout, 19, 173
Kennedy, Paul, 41
Kortright, Frank, 15, 82

Lake Simcoe, 104–5, 106
Lake trout, 91
Land O' Lakes District, 104, 210–11
Lateral sensory line on trout, 55,
123, 202–3
Leader, 88, 156–59
Line
double-tapered, 155–56
fly line, 154–56
freeing, 200
untwisting, 197–98
weight-forward, 155–56
Lox, 187, 190

Lures
  bait and, 61, 108, 114–15, 139,
    200–201
  Crocodiles, 149
    Delphin, 65, 199
    Gord Deval, 65–66, 199–200
  Daredevil, 66
  E.G.B., 62
  Flatfish, 28, 148, 182, 198, 199
  Halfwave, 62
  ice fishing, 113, 114
  Little Cleo, 199
  Mepps, 56, 58, 148, 182
  M.O.P. spoon, 54
  plugs, 56, 198, 199
  Rapala, 56, 113, 114, 130-31,
    148, 182, 198-99, 208, 209
  shell, 53–54
  spinners, 53–55, 56–62, 71,
    147–48, 197, 212
  sponge, 179–80
  spoons, 148–49
  Swedish Pimple, 114
  Vibrax spinner, 35, 56, 58, 148,
    182
  wobblers, 28, 53–55, 62–66, 108,
    199–200, 201, 212
  wooden, 55–56

Magder, Jesse, 139
Matching the hatch, 82, 83, 98, 203,
  204
Matusiak, Rick, 41–42, 112, 119, 149,
  209–210, 213–14
Ministry of Natural Resources, 25,
  26, 104
Mosque Lake, 54, 96
My Moby Dick, 138

Netting trout, 183–84
Nipigon River, 25, 64, 100
Noodle-rods-and-float-reel method,
  180, 181
Normark Canada, 56, 68, 113
Nottawasaga River, 139, 141–43
Nymphs, 89

O'Fishol, 139–44
Orpin, Bill, 212
Owens, Claude, 15

Pefferlaw Creek, 34
Perch, 96, 97
Pickerel, 49–50, 61, 65, 97, 215,
  219, 220
Pigeon River, 97
Pike, 65–66, 215, 216–19
Pokulok, Pete, 89–90, 96, 216–17
Polaroid glasses, 184–86
Port Credit harbour, 149

Rainbow trout
  bait, 20, 209
  coloration, 19, 176, 177, 219
  curing/smoking, 186–90
  diet, 174, 204, 208–9, 211
  drift fishing, 180–81
  fly-fishing, 193–95, 211–12
  habitat, 19–20, 172–73, 191, 192,
    195, 206–7, 208
  hatcheries, 20
  jigging, 196–97
  lures, 197, 198–99
  netting, 183–84
  size, 20
  spring-run
    bait, 178–80, 182

diet, 178–80
habitat, 186
lures, 182–83
spawning, 20, 173, 175, 177–78,
    185–86
temperament, 20, 205
trolling, 195–205
Rajeff, Steve, 79
Reddick, Dave, 14, 80
Reels, 4, 10, 61–62, 150, 172, 180,
    201–2
Rods, fly, 153–54, 162, 180, 181

Salmon, 102, 162, 173–74, 184,
    193, 204
Scarborough Fly and Bait Casting
    Association, 6, 61, 73, 78–79, 154
Schwartz, Leon, 155
Schwiebert, Ernest, 89
Senses, of trout, 55, 123, 151,
    202–3
Set lines, 16–17
Setting the hook, 42–43, 43–44,
    45, 52, 109, 195
Seychelles, Joe, 13
Sheldon Creek, 139, 141–43
Sludge Lake, 89
Smoking trout, 186–90
Spawn bags. See Roe bags
Stalking the Wild Asparagus, 187
Stark, Jim, 83, 96
Steelhead. See Rainbow trout,
    spring-run
Stocking programs, 25–26, 104,
    149, 173, 174
Strike indicators, 107–8, 195
Sutton, Jack, 15, 83
Swivels, 62–63, 108, 113, 209

Tailing, 184
Toronto Anglers and Hunters
    Association, 14, 15, 81
Trent River, 49
Trolling, 28, 58, 119, 148, 149,
    195–205
Trout, 168

Vibration, 57, 58, 109, 115, 123,
    129–30, 202, 203

Waders, 178
Walleye, 215
Walton, Izaak, 39, 129, 132, 147
Watercress, 42, 192, 219
Whittingham, Tony, 218
Wilkings, Doris, 67
Wilkings, Jack, 67–68, 69, 89–90, 115
Willowemoc River, 45, 145–46
Winisk watershed, 25
Wulff, Joan, 163, 164
Wulff, Lee, 15, 99–100, 162–67